Newspaper Sto

Old Geezer

Lonie B. Adcock

New book by local author Lonie B. Adcock honors area veterans

Posted: Tuesday, November 11, 2014 7:30 am

Local author Lonie B. Adcock hopes his new book will give recognition to the "little fellas."

"You go to a parade and you see the generals and they get lots of recognition," Adcock said. "But what about the others? The ones who didn't get noticed, but defended their country, came back home, started working and raising a family, those are the ones this book is for."

Adcock will sign copies of his book, "Tribute to the American Veterans" today from 1 to 4 p.m. at the Last Stop Gift Shop **on Jackson Hill**. The book is a hardback and costs $25, Adcock said.

The book is a collection of stories written by veterans and collected by Adcock, who also is a Rome News-Tribune columnist and a retired Rome police lieutenant.

"Some of the stories are just enough information to be short biographies," said Adcock. "But one fellow's story took 20 pages. My own story is in there, too."

Lonie Adcock

Lonie Adcock of Rome is a retired Rome Police Department lieutenant. His latest book, "More Memories of the Old Geezer," is now available.

More than 100 local veterans are represented in the book. Adcock said he sees it as a way to say thank you.

"One boy I talked to said he was 'just a cook' and never saw combat," said Adcock. "The way I look at it, you can't live without the cook. His story is important too."

LOCAL

Walker, Adcock win state honors

The writers for the Rome News-Tribune place in the Georgia Press Association 2015 Better Newspaper Contest.

om staff reports

The writings of Rome News-Tribune Associate Editor Doug Walker and columnist Lonie Adcock were recognized as among the top in the state by the Georgia Press Association.

Walker and Adcock won awards in the organization's 2015 Better Newspaper Contest. The GPA honored winners of the contest and the 2015 Freedom of Information Award during the group's 129th annual convention Friday.

Walker took third place for business coverage in the Division B Awards. First place went to Stuart Taylor of The Valdosta Daily Times

and second place went to Lindsey Adkison of The Brunswick News.

Adcock, a retired Rome police lieutenant and local author, won third place in the Division B humorous column category. First place went to Carlton Fletcher of The Albany Herald and second place went to Dick Yarbrough of the Marietta Daily Journal — whose column appears in the RN-T on Saturdays.

The Augusta Chronicle won the prestigious Freedom of Information Award for doing the most during 2014 to uphold the principles of the First Amendment and to protect the public's right to know. The Chronicle was honored

Doug Walker

Lonie Adcock

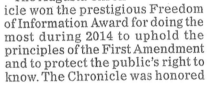
RN-T.com

Read this story online for a link to the Georgia Press Association website to see the complete list of winners.

for work on three separate stories — each requiring the determination of reporters to overcome roadblocks erected by government officials to close off information. Reporters Sandy Hodson, Travis Highfield, Tracey McManus and Tom Corwin covered the stories.

Contest entries were judged in eight divisions based on circulation. The daily newspaper divisions are Division A (circulation of 30,000 or more), Division B (8,000 to 29,999) and Division C (less than 8,000).

There were 616 awards presented in 36 categories to 78 newspapers.

GUEST COLUMNIST: Did 'Goot's ghost' help find suspect?

by LONIE ADCOCK, Guest Columnist

I WAS TALKING to Mike Ragland the other day about a house on South Broad that was supposed to be haunted. I wasn't sure about the exact location but I remember an incident, back many years ago. I always called the house on South Broad Goot's ghost. I remember that the house sat on the corner of a street that turned off of South Broad, just pass the old McCall Hospital. It sat up on a bank and you had to go up the street from South Broad to get to it. I believe that it is no longer there for it was torn down a while back.

There used to be a park at Myrtle Hill where the mausoleum is being built. Every Sunday the park would be full of boys and girls. There was a boy back then that used to come to the park who was called Goot. I remember that Goot had lost a leg and walked on crutches, but there weren't many who could out do him even if he had only one leg. The city swimming pool was at the end of Sixth Avenue close to the river. On Saturday you could find Goot there, climbing up on the diving board and doing flip-flops off of it.

I remember it as if it was yesterday and how I got into a situation that wasn't funny. I had an experience with a couple of my friends with a house that was on Branham Avenue, where the apartments now sit. I wasn't looking forward to another one. When you are young you don't know when you are well off, so you let your mouth over load you. It was a Sunday morning and the park was full of people. I sat on the bench with a few of my friends taking a ragging about ghosts.

IT SEEMED that some one had told about my experience in the house across the road from the park. I sat down and the first thing I knew was someone had slipped up behind me and yelled, "Boo." I jumped up and turning to see who it was, looking in to the face of Eddy, one of the boys who was with me that night. Some one, yelled" Eddy you scared him, look how pale he is." Eddy was a big joker and he was laughing so loud and hard that he had tears in his eyes. I didn't think it was so funny.

I looked toward the house across the road and a chill went up my back, and I turned and started to leave the park. That was when I saw Goot coming toward me. "Hey, Adcock," he said, "don't let these idiots get next to you." "Try to ignore Eddy the clown and the rest will leave you alone."

"Come on," he said going over to another bench and sat down. I sat down beside him and he began to talk," Adcock some people go though life, and never experience any thing more than being a jokester." " Eddy is one of them, when he does something to you, give him a sour look. If it doesn't bother you then it won't be funny to him and he will leave you alone." He got up saying, "Come on let's join the crowd."

We went over and sat down on a bench and every one gathered around to listen to what Goot had to say.

Goot looked the crowd over and began to laugh. "I bet, he said, that there is none among you who will go in one of those houses," and he pointed to them." All my life I have heard about the haunts in those houses.

"I WANT all of you who are so brave to come to a party at my house next Saturday night." He looked the crowd over. No one said any thing. He got up and said, "Next Saturday there will be a party at my house. We will play games and eat cake and ice cream. When it gets dark we will go inside, and I will let you meet my ghost."

He got up and smiled. "If those who laughed at Adcock are so brave, be at my house Saturday night at six." He put his crutch under his arm and left . Thinking back I am still amazed at how fast he could move.

Saturday came and out of curiosity I went to Goot's party to see who would come. I arrived to find the porch full of boys and girls. I look back and believe the reason that so many people came, was back then there were not too many things to do on a Saturday night. If you got the chance to go to a party you went. It was just getting dark so we began to play games. If you are old enough to remember back then you recall that the popular games to play were Post Office or Spin the Bottle. The night passed and Goot announced that the ice cream and cake were inside on the table.

"Oh yeah," he said "and Goot's ghost will be having cake and ice cream with us." A nervous smile and a silly giggle and everyone went inside. We entered a large hallway that had a table put up with chairs all around it.

A large piece of cake and a bowl of ice cream sat on the table. We filed in and sat down. Goot took a seat at the end of the table where we come in. This put him at the end where if any one decided to leave they would have to pass him. I was seated about half way down the table with a girl on either side of me.

I WILL ALWAYS remember Christine Wilkins, the one on my right. If she is still among us she will remember that night. "Dig in," Goot told us, "the ice cream is melting and the cake is growing old."

Everyone at the table began to eat. Goot began to spin his web of intrigue about his ghost. I watched the faces at the table. Some had theirs eyes wide open when he would mention ghosts. Goot was a good storyteller and I took in every word. So did Christine.

Goot's ghost story went this way: " It seems at certain times you could hear voices and foot steps in the hallway. If you didn't make any noise then it would move from the hallway and into the rooms. When all was over they would go up to the ceiling and make some more noise. Only there was no way to get up in the ceiling."

Goot said he would lay in bed at night and listen to the noises. He had got us all inside because it was about time for them to make their appearance. He looked around the table at every one and said, "Let's see how many of you will finish your cake and ice cream." With a smile on his face he began to eat.

I felt a cold chill go down my back and the hair on the back of my neck stood up. I don't know how it happened, but Christine had moved her chair so close that she was almost in my lap. A boy by the name of Johnny had grabbed up his cake and headed for the door. Several more boys and girls were already heading for the door. I sat still frozen to my chair.

Christine leaned over and whispered, "Can you see them?"

I DIDN'T SAY anything — I sat still. Things were happening all around the hallway. I know that there were noises, not made by the remaining few. Then with a yell that brought us all back, Eddy jumped to his feet. Jimmy was sitting beside him and when he jumped up, Eddy fell over Jimmy's chair. He was on his feet and out the door in just a few seconds.

Goot just sat there with a smile on his face.

This is one of those things that I have thought about through the years. Did Goot stage this to scare the ones who were making fun of me?

I know that cold chills and the hair stood up on the back of my neck happened that night. When we left Christine was holding my hand as if she would never turn it loose. There were sounds that sounded like whispering in the hallway. When they all had left and ran outside, I stood up and Goot smiled at Christine.

"Walk her home, Adcock," he said, "for she can't make it by herself." Christine lived on Third Avenue and all the way there she kept asking, "Did you see them, did you hear them." I remember keeping my mouth shut not answering her. I always believe that when there is doubt keep your mouth shut.

I had almost forgotten about what happened with Goot's ghost until talking to Mike.

In remembering, it brought back another incident that happened at that location.

I had been with the Police Department for a while. An officer by the name of Pete was my riding partner. At that time the family that lived in the house had a son named Billy Joe.

BILLY JOE would get to drinking and go home and his mother would call the police to come and get him out of the house. Pete and I got the call that Billy Joe was tearing up his mother's house and she wanted him out. We parked and went up on the porch and talked to his mother. We went inside where she said he had gone. We searched the house from end to end — no Billy Joe.

His mother came just inside the door and said he is in here for he hasn't come outside. Pete walked over to her saying, "We have looked everywhere. Is there a way up in the attic." She shook her head.

I was standing beside a couch that sat back in what I call an alcove. I had my back to it when a whispering voice said, "Couch." I turned to see who it was. No one was in the hall with me. Pete and the lady were standing in the door leading from the porch.

I walked over to the couch but it looked OK. I started to walk away when again I heard a whispered "Couch."

I motioned for Pete to come to me. He came and looked at the couch. "No way that anyone could be under there," he said.

I smiled and said, "Watch this." I faced the couch and with my 190 pounds jumped up on it.

A scream came from under the couch and I jumped back down to the floor. Billy Joe came from under the couch flipping it over. He stood up and in a drunk voice said, "How did you know I was under there."

"A little voice told me," I said, placing the cuffs on him.

AFTER thinking back, was Goot's ghost something he did or was it for real? If Christine was here she would say it was real.

Now the voice telling me Billy Joe was under the couch — was that imagination or was it real? As I have often stated there are things that I don't understand so I just move on but keeping them in my memories.

Lonie Adcock of Rome is a retired Rome Police Department lieutenant. His latest book, "Memories of an Old Geezer," is now available.

GUEST COLUMNIST: Merry Christmas at the Civic Center

Lonie Adcock, Guest Columnist | Posted: Friday, December 21, 2012 12:00 am

I was at the art fair, selling my book, when an incident that happened many years ago came to me. Back in the sixties, there was only two of us patrolling the city of Rome.

It was on a Christmas Eve when it happened, my regular partner was off that night, and the captain gave me a partner whom we all called Bookie. As some of the older police remember, Bookie smoked cigars. He kept one in his mouth about all the time. There is nothing quite as bad as a wet cigar in a closed car.

It was Christmas Eve, and everything was quiet. Most people were at home setting up Christmas for their little ones. Everything had closed at midnight, so when I first came on, I had gone by Krystal and picked up a couple of sandwiches. I had about all the wet cigar smoke I could take. I went up to the Civic Center where I was going to eat my sandwiches.

I made the turn on the lot from the road, and as I did I saw a movement in one of the windows. I gave the car the gas and drove up to where you go beside the building on the duck pond side. I jumped from the car and began to check the windows and the door. All was secure, and I went back to the car.

Bookie sat in the car puffing on the wet cigar. Bookie knew my name but never called me Lonie, it was always Lonzo.

"What you looking for Lonzo?" he asked.

"Santa Claus," I replied.

I made another round checking the windows and doors again. I couldn't find anything out of order so I went back to the car. I reached in and got my sandwiches from the seat and placed them on the hood. I started to eat, never taking my eyes off of the Civic Center. Bookie sat in the car puffing on his wet cigar.

I was looking at the window on the end of the building when I saw it again. I didn't say anything but walked over and looked into the building. Nothing moved, but I knew that I had seen someone or something move. I walked back over to the car and opened the door to get in and started to sit down but changed my mind. I reached and got the microphone.

I remember the conversation as if was yesterday.

"Car two to headquarters" I said.

"Go ahead car two" the dispatcher said.

"Headquarters call the city custodian and tell him to bring the keys to the Civic Center," I requested.

A slight hesitation then, "you know this is Christmas Eve?" I was beginning to get a little irritated with the radio and Bookie's wet cigar.

I remember with the irritation showing, I said "life goes on, tell Paul to get over here as soon as possible."

Car one, having no calls, pulled on to the lot. I went over to the car and told them what I had seen. They pulled to the end where they could see half of the Civic Center. I picked up my cold sandwich and coffee. I ate and drank coffee, smelling Bookies' wet cigar.

It seemed that Paul would never get there, but finally I saw his headlight as he came off of the road on the lot. I motioned for the officers in the other car to come with me to help search the building. I went through the door with the others behind me. We searched every corner of the building even looking in the refrigerator.

Nothing seemed to be out of place and no one could be found. The room had been set up for a party the next day. A Christmas tree was sitting in the front of the fireplace. Gifts were scattered around the tree. Sitting in the fire place was a bag of gifts. The bag looked out of place. The other officers had gone back to their car leaving Paul and I alone. That is all except Bookie with his wet cigar.

I started to go toward the door to leave when a thought came to me. I motion for Paul to wait.

"Bookie," I said pointing to the fire place.

A surprised look came on Bookie's face. He laid his cigar on a table and with his gun in hand we approached the fire place. I stepped to the side and pulled the sack from the fire place. Nothing was in the fireplace, it was empty. I remember that a thought came to me.

"Hey Paul," I said "is it okay if I shoot up this fireplace to make sure that no one is hiding in it?"

"Fire away," he yelled loud enough for everyone to hear.

A faint voice came from the fireplace, "don't shoot mister, I am coming down."

"Come out showing me empty hands!" I ordered.

I watched as a pair of shoes came into view, but I could not believe my eyes when the rest of him slid from the chimney. I will try to give you a description.

First, a pair of shoes that looked to be about 14 in size came into sight. Then, the shoes came sliding from inside the fireplace with the longest body attached to them that I have ever seen. He had to be over six feet tall and weighing less than one hundred pounds. I wanted to laugh but knew this was no laughing matter. He had soot all over him and with his hand sticking up in the air was the funniest sight I remember seeing.

"Face me," I said, "with your hands held high!" Bookie took his cuffs and put them on him. We led him out to the car and placed him in the back seat. In those days there were no cages in the car; when someone was placed in the back seat, someone got in with them.

Bookie started to get in then got out hollering at Paul. "Don't lock the door. I got to get my cigar!" He went back into the Civic Center and retrieved his wet cigar stub.

This fellow went by the name of Suge and in later years had half of the police department chasing him for burglary. He did time for the Civic Center burglary but came out and started up again. I always wondered if he thought he could get the big garbage bag up the chimney. The bag weighed as much as he did, if not more.

I know that old Santa Claus can carry a big bag of toys down the chimney, but I would just bet that a six foot fellow weighing less than a hundred pounds could not make it up the chimney with a bag of toys as big as Suge had.

Lonie Adcock of Rome is a retired Rome Police Department lieutenant. His latest book, "Memories of an Old Geezer," is now available.

GUEST COLUMN: The ghost bridge of Taylorsville

Lonie Adcock, guest columnist | Posted: Wednesday, January 15, 2014 7:15 am

There was one year while I lived on Reece Street in North Rome that two of my buddies and I must have visited every place in and around Rome that was supposed to be haunted.

Duke had a 1946 Hudson car. If you have ever seen one of them you know that you could put a car of today inside of it and have room to spare.

I was working in construction at the time. When I came off the job at about 1 p.m. one Saturday, Duke and Carlton were waiting for me. On the way home they told me that a bunch of the girls wanted to go ghost-hunting again.

It was around 6 p.m. when they came down to the house and got me. The car was full of girls. I opened the back door and, like a sardine in a can, squeezed in among them. I asked where we were going.

Lonie Adcock

Lonie Adcock of Rome is a retired Rome Police Department lieutenant. His latest book, "More Memories of the Old Geezer," is now available.

Francis, a girl who was always coming up with the places where ghosts were said to be, spoke up. "It's a bridge on the road that goes from Euharlee to Taylorsville," she said. "You can see ghosts on the bridge and hear them talking."

We got on the road to Euharlee and headed toward Taylorsville. The sun was still up and it was hot in the car. The only air you had back then was what we called open air. You rolled down the window and let the air in.

Along the road were signs saying "See Big Dan Cave Aragon Georgia." I had never been to Big Dan Cave and thought it would be something to do until it got dark enough to hunt ghosts. I suggested it and everyone thought it was a good idea.

On the way, we crossed a small bridge that was made with a poured concrete slab and a metal rail. I asked Francis, "Is that your ghost bridge?" As we were crossing it a cold chill went down my back. I knew without a doubt that this was the bridge.

We stopped at Big Dan Cave and looked around. It was more like a hole in a bank, if I remember, but in later years it turned out to be quite a place to take the family. I enjoyed it, but went back outside and talked to the lady who was running the place.

I asked her about the ghost bridge. She told me what I had thought: It was the small bridge that we had crossed. Then she began to tell me the story about why the bridge was haunted.

It seems that a young man and woman who lived in the area had been killed on the bridge. Their car had skidded on ice and hit the concrete. It had thrown the woman though the windshield and down into the creek. He had managed to get out and as he started for help she begged him not to leave her.

He was hurt badly but knew that she needed help. He assured her he would be back to get her. As he was leaving he could her crying "Please don't leave me." He arrived back with help to find she had died. It was told, but no one knew for sure, that he had died several days later.

The story was that she could be heard begging not to be left alone. In some cases it had been told that he could be seen on a moonlit night, searching for her along the creek bank under the bridge.

With a good story to tell the girls, we loaded up and went back to the bridge. It was beginning to get dark so we pulled off the road and waited. I told the story that the lady at Big Dan Cave told me but added a lot more to it.

I could feel the pressure of the girls crowding in on me as I told the story. I never cracked a smile and would let a break in my voice when stretching the fact about how you could hear him searching the creek bank under the bridge. We waited and it got dark and the moon shone though the clouds.

We all sat silently; it was so quiet you could hear yourself breathing. I had been to a lot of places that were supposed to be haunted. Some had gave me a surprise and some had not. I was about to give up on this place when there appeared what seem to be a light at the end of the bridge near the concrete.

I raised up to get a better view when one of the girls grabbed my arm. "Look," she said, pointing to the bridge. I heard a moan go though the car. The girls had seen it. Delores, a very small girl, would always get next to me. I accused her of getting in my pocket and hiding when we saw something. I eased the door open and, true to par, she was hanging on to me

I stood still beside the car and watched the light on the bridge. I reached down and found me a rock. I felt like some one was pulling a trick on us. With rock in hand, I moved slowly toward the bridge. I watched as the light disappeared beside the bridge. I stepped up on the bridge and looked down beside it at the creek bank. Nothing. I went to the other side. Nothing.

I know that there had been a light on the bridge. Where it went, I had no idea. Taking my penlight out of my pocket, I bent over and played the light under the bridge. There was nothing under the bridge that I could see. I heard a rustle in the bushes but didn't see what was causing it. I figured the rustling was some kind of animals under the bridge.

I turned to see where the others where. They stood at the edge of the bridge. I motioned for them to come out on the bridge and help me find the ghost. I placed my hands on the iron rail intending to lean over and look under the bridge again.

A voice came to me in a low, crying, moan. "Don't leave me. Please don't leave me." I straightened up and looked around to see if any of the others had tried to play a joke on me. They were still at the edge of the bridge looking at me.

"Are you going to stand there and not help me check out what that light was?" I asked. They came out to where I was and began to look around. As usual, Delores got next to me. I turned and placed my hands on the rail again. And I could not move, for again I heard, "Please don't leave me."

I looked at Delores. "Did you hear anything?" I asked. She shook her head, saying no. I took her by the hand and I will never know why I did what I did. I took her hands in mine and placed them on the rail. Again the voice. "Please don't leave." I looked down at Delores and saw a frightened face looking back at me.

"Did you hear something?" I asked. She pulled her hands from mine and began to back up with the others who had gathered in the middle of the bridge. I motioned for Francis to come to me. She came over with that "I am not afraid of anything" attitude. I reached out and took her by the hand saying, "Come let me hold your hand in the moonlight."

She took my hand and I moved her over to the rail. I reached my arms around her, placed her hands on the rail and she froze. I watched her as the voice again begged for help. She looked up at me and said, "You can hear things and now, with my hands in yours, I can hear it too." We stood and listened, being very still for there was a rustling under the bridge.

We finally loaded up and came back to Rome. We stopped off at Roy's and had something to eat. Everyone but Delores and Francis were jabbering as fast as they could. Delores was a quiet type of person but Francis was usually loud. She sat quiet and would look at me every now and then. We all agreed that the bridge didn't have any ghosts around it. We all agreed, that is, but Delores and Francis.

Lonie Adcock of Rome is a retired Rome Police Department lieutenant. His latest book is "More Memories of the Old Geezer."

GUEST COLUMN: We are all creatures made by God

By Lonie Adcock, Guest Columnist | Posted: Tuesday, February 11, 2014 6:35 am

I did a lot of thinking on this one before writing it. There are things that people do not like to see or read about. I felt that I would go ahead and write it up.

You see it on the news and in the paper all the time. I am talking about what people call those who have no place to live. They are called homeless, vagrants, bums and "too sorry to work." I met quite a few of them back when I was on the Rome Police Department

I walked a beat on Broad Street for several years. I got to know most of them by name and what had brought them to this stage in their life. I knew where they stayed at night, for most of them would come to the Cotton Block in the morning.

They would gather down at the end of the river bridge and wait to see if anyone would come along that needed someone to work. You could see them coming from under the bridges. That is where most of them lived. They had no homes or jobs, so they lived under the bridges or anywhere they could find shelter.

Lonie Adcock

Lonie Adcock of Rome is a retired Rome Police Department lieutenant. His latest book, "More Memories of the Old Geezer," is now available.

Most of them were alcoholics and stayed drunk most of the time. There was one that I remember and will not forget. He was a black man and his name was Louis.

Louis lived under the Second Avenue Bridge with a white man by the name of Irvin. They had built a house under the bridge out of cardboard boxes. They had a wood heater that only had one leg on it. The other sides sat on bricks. They gathered wood crates from the back of the stores and carried them under the bridge and made beds out of them. With their wood stove and homemade beds, they had a board that lay on bricks for a table.

The first time I went there I was surprised at what I saw. It was not what I wanted to live in, but it beat being out in the weather on a cold gray day. They built it back against the concrete pillar that helped keep the wind from hitting it. I remember laughing when Irvin called it a hacienda overlooking the water of the Coosa.

One day I got a call that a man was in the river. I headed for the Second Avenue bridge. When I pulled in at the bridge, Louis pointed toward the water. I got to where I could see and there, laying half in the river and half out, was Irvin.

This was a steep bank and I explained to headquarters what I had. With an ambulance en route, I worked my way to where Irvin lay. He never moved. In my mind he was dead, but just as I bent over to check him, he let out a moan. I noticed that he had ice all over his clothes where he had gotten wet.

The ambulance arrived and the EMTs began their chore to get to us. I motioned to one of the EMTs and he bent over and felt for Irvin's pulse. He straightened up and said, "this man should be dead but he is still alive."

Irvin was a big man and it took five of us to get him up the bank to the ambulance. At the hospital, the doctor who examined him shook his head and said, "he should be dead but he has so much alcohol in him that it has kept him alive." I went to police headquarters and made out a report. Several weeks later I saw Irvin sitting on a porch in West Rome. How he had survived, I often wondered.

I would take a hot cup of coffee and an egg sandwich to Louis on an occasion. I would pull in and blow the horn and he would come out and get the coffee and sandwich. I kept a check on Louis for quite a while.

It was on a cold wet day I was flagged down by a person who advised me that something was wrong with Louis. I went to the bridge and got out. I walked down to the hacienda, as Irvin called it, pushed open the wooden door and looked in. I knew when I saw him that he was dead. Louis had frozen to death.

I have always tried not to judge anyone. I do not qualify as a judge. Everyone will be judged, when the time comes, by a qualified judge.

I remember that Irvin lived for several more years after falling into the river. As I stated, I have heard them called all kind of names. It does not matter whether you live in a mansion, drive a Cadillac or live under a bridge. When the time comes, you will be judged. All of us are creatures made by God.

Lonie Adcock of Rome is a retired Rome Police Department lieutenant. His latest book is "More Memories of the Old Geezer."

GUEST COLUMN: Back to the haunted bridge

By Lonie Adcock, Guest Columnist | Posted: Tuesday, March 18, 2014 6:30 am

I had said to myself that there are certain things that I would not write about. There are things in life that are hard to understand. If you talk about it there are some people who will say, "boy, is this guy a nut." Nut or not, here goes, back to the Haunted Bridge.

After the visit to the bridge, the girls didn't say too much about going ghost hunting for a few weeks. Francis was the main one in much of the ghost hunting. I didn't go to the park the next week for I was working a lot of overtime. I usually saw Francis at the park with the rest of the girls. I remember that I didn't see Duke or Carlton that week either.

Then we got caught up on the job and things settled down, so back to the park with the crowd.

I was sitting on a bench with a book when Francis came over and sat down. She looked at me and said "hey." I sensed that something was bothering her. I

Lonie Adcock

Lonie Adcock of Rome is a retired Rome Police Department lieutenant. His latest book, "More Memories of the Old Geezer," is now available.

had learned to read the crowd of girls at the park like a book. "Give," I said. "What is bugging you?" She looked at me kind of funny and said, "my mama wants to see you."

"What does your mama want" I asked. She stood up and looked down at me. "Coming?" she asked. "Why not," I said, getting up.

On the way to her house I remember asking "what have you been telling your mother?" She was quiet so I didn't ask her anything else. I went into the house and her mother and father were sitting on the couch. Her father pointed to a chair. "Have a seat, son," he said. I sat down facing them. Francis sat down in a chair beside me. She looked miserable when I looked at her.

When you looked at those two, you knew that you were looking at two full-blooded Cherokee Indians. "Well," I said. "You didn't get me up here just to look at me, so go ahead and get whatever it is off your mind." Francis' father spoke first. "Son," he said. "This is my wife's idea so I will let her tell you what she wants."

As close as I can remember it went like this:

It seems that, unknown to most people, Francis' mother was a psychic. When she said that Francis had told her about the haunted bridge, it had bothered her. Her way of thinking was that a soul was tied to the bridge that needed releasing so that it could go home to rest.

This threw me, for I had no knowledge of what a psychic was or could do. I looked at Francis as her mother spoke. It seemed that her mother wanted us to take her to the bridge so she could speak to the lost souls. I was almost to the point of getting up and leaving when she said, "I will bestow good vibes on you, if you will get your buddy to take us to the bridge. You must tell him that what he sees he cannot tell anyone."

On my way back to the park I got to wondering what in the heck was a vibe. There had been no time in my life, at that time, that I had come across a psychic. I was glad that she had decided to sent good vibes my way for I had enough bad things happen in my lifetime.

I stopped and told Duke what Francis' mother wanted. He sat silently. Then he said, "the only time I ever saw her mother it sent chills down my back." I waited to see what he was going to do. He asked me if I had ever been to a psychic. "No," I said. He proceeded to tell me about the power of psychics and the power they had to talk to the dead. I waited. Finally he said, "tell her we will take her and Francis back to the bridge."

I left and went home. I had to get up early in the morning and go to work. I remember that night was one of tossing and turning. I got up the next morning and felt like I had worked all night. How I made it through that day I will never know. Somehow I did, and that evening I went back to the park. Francis was there and I told her to tell her mother we would pick them up Saturday night at six.

Saturday evening, at about 5:30 p.m., Duke came down to the house and picked me up. Francis lived on what was called Roseway Circle, which was on the hill at the end of Callahan Street. We pulled up in front of her house and they came out and got in the car. Everyone was quiet until Francis' mother spoke, "I ask that neither one of you boys tell a living soul what you see and hear tonight." Sworn to silence by her, Duke and I didn't have much to say.

The ride to the bridge seem to take forever with the silence in the car. We were used to all kind of talking when the girls were in the car. It wasn't quite dark enough when we got to the bridge so we killed time at Big Dan Cave.

The night was dark, the moon was hidden behind a cloud. We parked in the same place as we were before. I opened the door and stepped out to find Francis' mother was already at the edge of the bridge. I took my penlight out and went to where she had stopped. "Which rail did you touch," she asked. I pointed to the concrete slab where the rail was "Come," she said, and walked over to the rail.

I heard a rustle in the weeds under the bridge. She was standing with her hands stretched out toward the rail. I stopped still. She was talking ,but I couldn't hear what she was saying. I touched the rail out of curiosity, and again the voices could be heard. I stepped back away from the rail. In backing up I bumped into Francis, who was standing still with an odd expression on her face.

I have no idea how long we stood there watching her. She seemed to be saying a prayer of some kind but I could not make out what she said. The moon came from behind the clouds and the bridge lit up like daylight. I heard a noise come from Francis and Duke at what they saw. I can't say what we saw, except that it looked like two figures floating in thin air. The mist or whatever it was disappeared in the night. Francis' mother came over and said, "I am ready to go."

We drove the women home and went back uptown to the Krystal and ate a hamburger. We sat at the stools at the back wall and talked about what had happened and what we had seen. We went home early and I went to bed. It was another one of those nights of tossing and turning.

I never talked to anyone except Francis and Duke about this.

When I would go to Francis' house her father would call me "son." The others he would call by name. When I asked Francis why, she said "Daddy sees the Cherokee in you." I talked to her mother, and she would only say, "there are two lonely souls back together and waiting for judgment day in heaven."

Lonie Adcock of Rome is a retired Rome Police Department lieutenant. His latest book is "More Memories of the Old Geezer."

GUEST COLUMN: Baby it's cold outside

By Lonie Adcock, Guest Columnist | Posted: Tuesday, April 15, 2014 6:30 am

With the kind of weather we've had this year, it brings back memories of another winter. Unlike this one, it was in Germany. It was nothing for it to get below zero there, especially at night. We complain about the cold weather in the winter and the hot weather in the summer. You cannot please all the people all the time — it is hard to please some of them some of the time.

New York, 1951, the 315 Signal Construction Battalion was about to embark on a long journey. This would be a journey that would not soon be forgotten. It was a journey to Germany; for how long, we were not sure. We had a great time seeing New York, but all good things must end.

We fell out at three o'clock in the morning. A trip to the mess hall. After breakfast we went back to the barracks. There we got our barracks bags, along with other equipment, and they loaded us on to army trucks. We left Camp Kilmer, N.J., headed for Staten Island.

Lonie Adcock

Lonie Adcock of Rome is a retired Rome Police Department lieutenant. His latest book, "More Memories of the Old Geezer," is now available.

It wasn't a long trip and we got to see more of New York. We were unloaded and placed in an area where a band was. As we marched in, the band played "Dixie." We were an all-Southern outfit. Several more tunes and we began to load aboard a ferry to Staten Island. It was there that we saw the Statue Of Liberty. I thought that was the most beautiful thing that I had ever seen. I didn't realize just how beautiful she was until later.

No time was lost — they unloaded us from the ferry and onto a big ship that was at a pier. This was a troop transport ship that also carried dependents. Half of the ship was loaded with soldiers' dependents and the other half was ours. We, the soldiers, would not cross a line that was on the ship's deck. It was with the understanding that if you were caught over the line you would make the rest of the journey in the brig at night, KP during the day. I looked the line over to make sure that I never crossed it. We were hustled to where we would be sleeping for the journey. I was on the second deck, in a hammock under the stairs.

Early the next morning we were told that after breakfast we could go up on deck. I went up and went to the side that showed Miss Liberty in all her glory.

We sailed out of the harbor around noontime. I had no idea how long it would take to get to Germany. I had rather gone back to Georgia. The trip was a long one to me. We docked in England and let off some dependents. The next stop was Bremerhaven, Germany.

We came off the ship and were loaded onto a train. We were given a brown sack with sandwiches in it. That was to be our lunch, eat sparsely. The train looked like something you would see in a movie. The compartment sat four people with seats and an overhead pull-down for sleeping.

We went through the mountains at what seemed a snail's pace. We pulled into a village and the train was side-tracked, They brought us some more cold sandwiches. Early next morning more sandwiches, and then aboard trucks.

The top was down and it began to snow.

We headed for the mountains. We went through a town called Pirmasens. The camp was on the other side of town, on a hill. The ground was covered with snow and we were about to freeze. They put us in barracks and, as cold as it was, we were ordered to take showers. I nearly froze to death — the water was ice cold. There is nothing as refreshing as a ride though zero-degree weather in the back of a truck with the top off and, when you arrive, a cold shower. Try it sometime.

The next day our equipment arrived and that meant standing guard duty. The motorpool was on top of a mountain, about a mile from the camp. We had to have 24-hour guards at all times. It sure did get cold in those mountains at night. I told the Sergeant of Guards, "if I fall down I have so many clothes on that it would take a crane to pick me up."

I found out later that it was warm there, compared to where we would go before returning home.

We were on what was called the Ziegfeld Line. Gen. George Patton had gone thorough there with the Third Army. We had Third Army patches on everything, including our shoulders. We had to change them to the Seventh Army patches. We were there for about a month when we were ordered to pack up, we were moving out.

We came down out of the mountains to the Rhine River Valley. The temperature made a change that was hard to believe. It was like leaving Georgia in the middle of winter and going to Florida. We moved in to a camp in Worms. We had nice brick buildings and there were two other outfits there. One was an armored division; the other was a WAC — Women's Army Corps — detachment.

We felt like we had been sent to heaven, but the worst was yet to come.

With all our equipment spic and span, we settled in to take life easy. Orders came: We were to take part in the biggest maneuvers ever. Can you guess where we were ordered to? A town close to the

Russian border by the name of Wildflicken. We loaded up and headed out, and the closer we got to the Russian border, the colder it was. We stayed in those mountains around Wildflicken close to a month. There was a base there, but we had to sleep and live in the field.

It was cold during the day, colder at night. We would run the truck engines until the manifold got hot. We put our C rations on it to get them warm. We filled our cups with snow to make our coffee.

One night, I went to sleep rolled up in my sleeping bag and thought I was going to freeze to death. I had gotten in a small ditch so the wind would not hit me. I got warm and went to sleep but when I woke up I couldn't see a thing. I pulled my arm from inside the sleeping bag to find I was covered in snow. It had snowed during the night, covering me up in the ditch. I worked my way out and stood up. I was surprised to everyone was up and moving around.

The sergeant told me they had been trying to find me.

I will never forget it — for it was the first of December — when we finally started down out of those mountains. Snow was piled on the side of the road so high that you couldn't see what was on either side. As we approached the Rhine River Valley, it begin to warm up. When we arrived back at camp it was like being on a vacation.

I can't remember ever being as cold as I was in those mountains in Germany. We settled in and began to live again. We didn't know that our Uncle Sam had another surprise waiting for us. It was after Christmas that the orders came through: back to the mountains. We spent another miserable month in the cold. When we came down out of the mountains that time, we never had to go back again.

It's been cold here this winter and we are not used to it.

Be thankful that you don't have six months of this cold weather. I was in those mountain in the springtime and it was still cold. The mountains would be cold, but down in the Rhine River Valley the cherry trees would be blooming and the men would have on their leather shorts.

Lonie Adcock of Rome is a retired Rome Police Department lieutenant. His latest book is "More Memories of the Old Geezer."

COLUMN: A very strange bedfellow indeed

Lonie Adcock, Guest Columnist | Posted: Tuesday, June 24, 2014 8:30 am

In my years of being a policeman I answered a lot of strange calls. I have hunted everything from ghosts to snakes — even chased bears around town. Once I had a chase with a monkey.

I have seen and heard about all of the things that make people call the police.

It was on a cool night when dispatch gave Car One a call to a subdivision off Burnett Ferry Road. This was a new subdivision, all the houses were new. People were moving into the subdivision as soon as a house was completed. It was a beautiful area, and the yards of the houses were beautiful. It was an early spring night; warm days, cold nights.

I was on Shorter Avenue when the call came in. I decided to cruise on out and see what kind of problem they were having in such a beautiful subdivision.

The officer checked out as I turned onto Burnett Ferry Road. I turned into the subdivision just as the

Lonie Adcock

Lonie Adcock of Rome is a retired Rome Police Department lieutenant. His latest book, "More Memories of the Old Geezer," is now available.

officer asked for a supervisor. I told him I was close and would be there in a few minutes. I pulled up in front of the house, checked out of service, and got out of the car.

I walked up on the porch and was met by the officer. We stopped on the porch, and he began to tell me what was the problem. He said what it sounded like to him was that the lady had a ghost in her house.

He gave me a big smile and said, "Lieutenant, this is right down your alley." I didn't say anything for the lady was close, and I didn't want to hurt her feelings by making a remark. I went into the house, and she began to explain her problem.

She said that she would go to work in the morning and come back home to find her garbage spilled out on the floor. She stated that she had no dog or cat in the house. To make matters worse, she felt like something was sleeping on the bed with her at night.

I found out that just recently her husband had passed away. I felt like that could be some of the problem. I talked to her and asked if she would like for us to search her house to see if there was anyone hiding inside. She wanted us to search so we went through the house giving it a good search — nothing.

Having satisfied her that there was nothing in her house, we left. I met the officer at a car wash on Shorter Avenue, and we talked about her problem. We could find nothing that would scatter her garbage on the floor. There was no one else in the house.

The officer laughed and said "Lieutenant, do you remember the house on Fourth Avenue?" I remembered the house on the hill all right, I would never forget it. I laughed and pulled out onto Shorter Avenue. The rest of the night went quietly, and we got off and went home.

The next night I had just got on the road when dispatch said the lady where we had been the night before wanted to see the officers. I told the car on the beat I would meet him there. When I got there the other officer had already checked out.

I went in to where the lady and the officer were. I followed them into the kitchen. Garbage was scattered all over the floor. All the doors were locked, and none of the windows were broken. I walked the outside over, and everything was OK. I went back inside; she had cleaned up the garbage and was mopping the floor. We went into the living room and sat down.

I found out that she went to work at 3 in the evening and got off at 11 o'clock. She always made sure that all the windows and doors were secure. She had no one who had keys to her house. We sat there for a period of time discussing what could it be. She kept talking about how Otis, her husband, could have come back. I assured her that there were no ghosts in her house.

As we started to leave she looked at me and said, "Officer, there are strange things happening to me. I want to know what it is." I told her we would do all we could to help her find what it was. As I stepped outside of the door, she said, "Crazy or not, something or someone is sleeping with me at night." As I drove back to Shorter Avenue I thought about what she had said.

We changed shifts and went on the evening shift. I heard an officer talk about a crazy woman who had boogers sleeping with her. I knew that the woman was not crazy but frightened. I went out through the subdivision, just looking around. I passed the house where we had gotten the call, and she was out in the yard. She was trimming some rose bushes. I pulled up and got out of the car. She looked up, and when she recognized me a big smile came on her face.

I had never been to her house in the daylight, and the house and yard were beautiful. I started to talk to her, to find out if she was still having problems. She stated that now she could hear someone or something walking in the house. She would turn on the light and could find nothing.

I asked her if she would mind if I and the other officer checked her house again. She let me know how delighted she would be if we would. I called the officer who had been there with me before.

With flashlights in hand we began a search of the house. We went over the house with a fine-tooth comb. Nothing. We stood in the doorway looking at each other when she said "it still sleeps with me."

That rang a bell in my head. I headed back to her bedroom. The only place that we had not looked was under the bed. I pulled up the cover to where I could see under the bed. I lay down on the floor and shone my light under the bed. I could not believe what I was looking at. I motioned for the other officer to look under the bed. He shone his light, then began to laugh.

He stood up and said "the Lieutenant has found your problem." He bent over and got a hold of the culprit. There was a hissing sound, and he pulled out the fattest opossum I had ever seen. He held it by the tail to where the lady could see it. He then carried it outside and put it down. He stepped back inside, and the opossum tried to get back in the house.

We all got a good laugh, including the woman whose house the opossum had made his home. We walked back to the car, and the officer said to me, "Tonight I am going to tell that other officer who called that lady a crazy woman something that he will not forget."

As I had come out the door, the opossum tried to get back in the house again. I had called him Harry and said, "Not tonight."

It was several weeks later that I was riding though the subdivision when I saw the lady out in her yard. She was on the curb working on her flowers. I pulled up, and she gave me a big smile and said "Officer, if you have time I would like to show you something." I checked out and followed her around the house to the backyard.

She opened a screen door that was on a small room. She called it her tool room. There in a corner of the room was a small house. On the front of it, written on a tag and placed on the house, was a sign that said "HARRY." A bowl of food with water sat beside it. She knocked on the top of the house and said "Harry, you lazy thing, come out here."

I stepped back to where I could see what Harry was. I started to laugh for through the door of the small house came the head of a opossum. She had made it a house and gave it food and water. As I was leaving I asked her why she called it Harry. "Why," she said, "I thought that is what it was. I remember you called it a Harry." I couldn't help laughing for she thought the opossum was an animal called a Harry.

Whether it was a Harry or an Opossum, I bet it was the only one who had a house of its own, with a human to wait on it. Did Harry not live the life of Riley?

Lonie Adcock of Rome is a retired Rome Police Department lieutenant. His latest book is "More Memories of the Old Geezer."

GUEST COLUMN: Old Jim the Fisherman

By Lonie Adcock, Guest Columnist | Posted: Tuesday, July 22, 2014 6:30 am

As you turn off South Broad Street onto Branham Avenue, there, across from the cemetery, were two houses. I had noticed that there was a trail between the houses that went down to the riverbank. The houses had people living in them.

I would go down to the playground and would look at the river. To get to the river you would have to go though their yard. We were taught to never go around anyone's house without their permission. I wanted to go fishing in the fork of the river. The trail between the houses seemed to be the best way to get there.

With fishing pole and bait in hand, I walked up on the porch and knocked. The door opened an old black gentleman opened the door. "Yes?" he said. I explained to him that I would like to come though his yard to get to the river. He smiled. "Going to get one of them big old catfish?" he asked. "Yes, sir," I said. He said, "Come on around to the back yard. I will show you some red worms you won't believe."

Lonie Adcock

Lonie Adcock of Rome is a retired Rome Police Department lieutenant. His latest book, "More Memories of the Old Geezer," is now available.

I picked up my pole and went around to the back yard. I could see the trail going to the river. He came out with a can in his hand. "Over here," he said, going over to what looked like a bathtub buried in the yard. He picked up a fork and turned the soft dirt. There were some of the biggest red worms I had ever seen. He had a worm bed in a bathtub.

He smiled. "Feed them good and they will get fat." Then he asked, "You don't mind if I go with you?" "No sir," I said. "I would like that. I don't like to fish by myself." He picked up a fancy rod and reel from the back porch. Smiling, he said, "Come on boy, let's go get us a big catfish for supper."

He led the way with me following closely. I looked at the fancy rod and reel, wishing I could get me one. I couldn't afford it, so I would have to use my cane pole. I had a good cane pole. It was seasoned by the sun and was extra tough. I had caught a lot of fish with it. I followed him down to the riverbank close to the water.

There were some old rusty pieces of iron and other pieces of metal sticking out of the mud. I went around to a willow tree growing out over the water. He watched me, and when I got situated where I wanted, he walked down to the pieces of metal and threw out. I put my line in.

I had ahold of the pole when the fish hit. With a good hardy yank, I caught the first catfish. I remember him laughing, saying, "Man, I done gone and got me a real fisherman for a buddy."

We fished until around noon. I told him I had to go. I had a nice string of catfish. He had caught a big one, and we laughed when he almost slid in the river. Assuring him that I would be back the next Saturday, I left.

I looked forward to the next Saturday, for I had found a catfish hole. When we were young and fished a lot, we would look for what we called a catfish hole. It was a place where it seemed to always be full of catfish. I was not going to tell anyone about it.

I had found out that his name was Jim. He lived there with his daughter. He was retired, and fishing was his favorite pastime.

Jim's last name was Whatley, and his daughter was Doris. Two finer people I have never known. Jim and I would come off the riverbank tired and hungry; Doris would have a sandwich and a cup of coffee waiting for us. She always said, "you two fishermens wash up and get the mud off of your feet." When we went in she would have food of some kind on the table. I would sit and talk to Doris, for when we came in from fishing Jim would go to bed. I found out he had a heart condition that made him get tired real fast.

I did a lot of fishing that year with Jim. I would go fishing every time I had a chance. I remember that I was 15 years old and working in construction. The weekends were about the only time I had a chance to go. Then I had to work on several weekends and didn't have a chance to go fishing.

When I finally got the chance again, I grabbed my pole and headed for Jim's house. I turned off of South Broad onto Branham Avenue and stopped — for sitting in front of Jim's house was a moving van. I walked slowly up to the front porch. The house was almost empty. Doris came to the door and saw me. She came to me with tears in her eyes. I told her that I had been working and couldn't get over to go fishing with Jim.

She reached out and hugged me, with tears in her eyes. "Dad died two weeks ago," she said. I don't think I have ever had anything to hit me like that. I sat down on the porch. She sat down beside me. We talked for a while.

She kept on thanking me for bringing some fun into her father's life. She said he talked about his Little Fishing Buddy. She got up and went inside the house. She came out with Jim's fancy rod and reel in her hands. She came over to me and handed it to me. "I believe Dad would have wanted you to have this." I took it, handling it very gently.

I watched as the truck pulled out with her in it. She had said she was moving to Tifton, Georgia, where most of her people lived.

I kept the reel for many years.

The rod had gotten broken while fishing. The reel stopped working. But I kept it because it had belonged to Jim. It lay on a table in my room for many a year. While I was in the Army my room was broken into and along with other stuff the reel was taken.

Lonie Adcock of Rome is a retired Rome Police Department lieutenant. His latest book is "More Memories of the Old Geezer."

GUEST COLUMN: The big bird scare

By Lonie Adcock, Guest Columnist | Posted: Wednesday, August 27, 2014 6:30 am

I was watching a cartoon in the dentist office while waiting for my wife. A scene with a lot of animals came on, and in it was a group of some of the most awful birds that I had ever seen. They ranged in size from small to large. From ugly to disgusting. It brought back an incident that happened back in the sixties.

Lonie Adcock

I was called to see one of my units on Cotton Avenue, which is down close to the river in East Rome. The woods come right up to the streets. We were always getting calls about strange animals in that area. I was told by one old fellow who had lived there all his life that he had seen a werewolf along the river.

I checked out of the patrol car and went to the back yard where the officers were. They were talking to a very small old lady. One of the officers came over to me and said, "We will take a report but what she says in unbelievable." I walked over to

Lonie Adcock of Rome is a retired Rome Police Department lieutenant. His latest book, "More Memories of the Old Geezer," is now available.

the officer talking to the lady and he said, "This is my supervisor, tell him what you saw."

I listened as the old lady began to speak. It went something like this:

It seemed that she had heard a noise in her back yard. She went out to see what it was. There in her garden was the biggest bird that she had ever seen. It stood a good six feet tall, with a long neck and a small head. It had a funny-looking beak. When she tried to shoo it out of her garden it came running toward her. She ran in the house and called the police.

I listened to her and watched her face as she talked. I could see that what she had seen had scared her.

I walked back around in front of the house to where the other officer stood. "Well, Lieutenant, what do you think?" I shook my head, saying, "I have no idea what she saw. Whatever it was it scared her. Come on, let's look around and see if there are any tracks or anything it left behind."

We walked down the road to the woods. We started back when the other officer reached down and picked up a feather from the ground. We looked at it but didn't know what kind of bird had lost it. It was a feather like I had never seen before. He held the feather, and we looked at it. "You don't suppose that the old lady really saw a bird as big as she said?"

I shook my head, not knowing or having any idea what she had seen.

Back in the patrol car, I started down Hardy Avenue. I was flagged down by a young boy on a bicycle. He was all excited, I calmed him down and found out he was in the woods when he came up on a big bird. He had started back toward Hardy Avenue when it saw him. It ran after him until he got out of the woods.

I called the other patrol car, telling them what the young boy had said. I went up to the spot where he said he had seen the bird. The other car came up, and we searched the area. We found nothing that would indicate that a big bird was in the area. I went in to the station and signed out my shift for the day.

I went in the next morning to find that the second shift had received several calls the day before on the big bird. I left out from the station, thinking this will be one of them days when you run yourself crazy trying to find a six-foot bird with a long neck.

It was quiet for a while before the calls on the giant bird began to come in. I was on Broad Street when the first call came in. I headed to where the bird had been seen. I got there and realized that it was the woods behind the Coosa Country Club. I went down into the woods as far as I could get. Stopping the car, I got out. I heard something in the bushes and walked over to get a look.

There he stood, all six feet of him with his long neck. I laughed to myself, thinking the old lady was right. I called for the other car to come to where I was. It wasn't just a few minutes before they pulled in. I motioned for them to be quiet but to come to where I was.

I pointed to the big bird, who was busy eating some kind of grass. "How are we going to get him?" one of the officers asked. I called headquarters to tell them what we had. They got in touch with Animal Control, who sent someone to try to capture the bird.

When they got there I was surprised to see one of them take out a rope. The bird was not paying any attention to us. He was busy having his breakfast. The Animal Control officer walked over and tossed the rope over his head. That brought on something else.

He went wild, but the officer held the rope until he settled down. They opened the back of the truck and put in a pan of grain. It was like leading a baby to ice cream. He walked into the truck and began to eat.

With the big bird in custody I went down to the lady's house on Cotton Avenue and told her that we had captured it. We talked for a few minutes then I left. I assured her that we hadn't thought she was crazy when she was telling us about the big bird. It had sounded like a science fiction story.

When I looked at the big bird there in the woods I had gotten a good laugh. Stop and think what you would do if you had never seen an ostrich and here come one running at you. I know exactly what I would do. I would move out as fast as possible, heading for greener pastures.

Lonie Adcock of Rome is a retired Rome Police Department lieutenant. His latest book is "More Memories of the Old Geezer."

GUEST COLUMN: Do not eat the eggs

Posted: Tuesday, September 2, 2014 7:15 am

I was thinking back on an incident that happened years ago. It was an Easter Sunday and I had come downtown to see what was going on.

I got there in the middle of people wearing some of the fanciest clothes of that time.

Older women wearing beautiful dresses that dated back to the old days, young girls all fancied up in their pretty clothes — and in among all those fancy duds was a poor boy wearing jeans, a pullover and a pair of cowboy boots. To make matters worse the pullover shirt was a bright red. It stood out in the crowd.

I ignored the stares that I was getting and strolled in among all the fancy clothes with a big smile on my face.

The boots were of a dark burgundy color. It was the prettiest pair of boots I had ever seen.

Lonie Adcock

Lonie Adcock of Rome is a retired Rome Police Department lieutenant. His latest book, "More Memories of the Old Geezer," is now available.

I was working in construction at that time. A pawn shop had the boots in the window and when I got paid that Friday I went in and bought them. They were the most expensive pair of boots that I had ever owned. They had cost me three dollars and a half. I had worked on them and they looked liked a mirror.

I can't recall ever having any type of footwear that shined like those boots. Back in those days, the boys got their jeans too long so that they could turn them up a cuff. I can honestly say that all those people who wore the fancy clothes did not strut half as much as I did in my shiny boots.

I sat on a bench where the buses stopped. I marveled at the people in their fancy clothes. The women in their bright-colored dresses and the men in their fancy suits. I heard two people talking about the parade. I had missed the parade but was getting an eyeful just sitting on the bench watching.

After a while I got bored watching the people strut by. I got up and started down the street to see what was going on at the lower end of Broad. I noticed the people going across the bridge to South Broad. I mingled with the crowd and followed them to the park on Branham Avenue.

The park was full of people. A table was set up at the entrance of the park, and as people went in they were given a basket.

I backed off and watched as the people came in to the park. I could see that it appeared to be an Easter egg hunt. The basket was to put the eggs in when they found them. I knew that it was a private affair and me and my jeans would not be welcome.

I turned to leave when I heard someone call my name. I turned around and, to my surprise, saw a girl who I went to West Rome School with.

Standing there with a big smile on her face was a girl that I hadn't seen in years. I knew her when I saw her, for she always had a big smile on her face.

She came over to me and started to talk. We moved out of the line of people going into the park and sat down on a wall. I found out where all of the old group of boys and girls that I went to West Rome School with were. Most of them were still in school.

Most of the people were in the park and I got up to leave. Jo Ann, the girl who was with me, got up and said, "Come on." I shook my head, saying, "Hey, this is a private party and I am not part of the group that belongs to it."

She reached out and took my hand and began to pull me. I followed her past the table and into the park. I could feel the eyes on me. I whispered that I should leave, for it might get her in trouble. As we went by the table she picked up a basket. We went over to a well-dressed woman and a man. She introduced me to them — her mother and father.

They gave me one of those looks. Her mother took her aside and I could see that she was laying down the law to her.

I seized the opportunity and headed for the entrance of the park to make an exit. A hand grabbed my arm just as I reached the table. I turned to look into Jo Ann's face. The smile that was usually on her face was gone.

I continued to walk even as she pulled on my arm. Just outside of the park I turned to her. She had tears in her eyes. "You were always my friend in school," she said. "Come back with me, and we will go Easter eggs hunting, whether they like it or not."

I went back into the park and went Easter egg hunting with her.

The man at the table kept telling everyone not to eat the eggs, for there were three that were worth money. I would pick up an egg and put it in the basket. I watched the people. I could see that I was an unwelcome person. I got to feeling miserable with all the eyes on me. I explained to Jo Ann and she understood.

They were going though the eggs to find the ones that were marked for the prize. I walked to where the table sat and moved around it outside of the park. Jo Ann came out with me. "Here," she said, and handed me an egg. I looked around. No one was watching. I took the egg and headed toward South Broad.

I sat down on a bench that was a bus stop and watched the people strut around. I began to get hungry so I took the egg that Jo Ann had gave me and looked at it. A smile came to my face, then I started to laugh.

The egg that she gave me was the egg that had the grand prize marked on it.

I gently cracked it and pulled the shell off. I took a bite. I believe this was the best egg that I ever ate. I sat there and ate the prize egg as the people in the park hunted for it. Feeling good, I got up and started back up Broad Street, watching the people in their fancy clothes.

I look back and know that I should have carried the prize egg back to them. But I remember the look on Jo Ann's face and think maybe that was her way of getting even with her parents.

I knew that when I entered the park I was out of my class. I knew that I was not welcome. I knew that I was being judged by the people in the park.

I often wondered if the people who judged me realized that a day would come when they would be judged. It was Easter and that should have meant something to those who judged a poor boy by his looks.

Lonie Adcock of Rome is a retired Rome Police Department lieutenant and regular columnist for the Rome News-Tribune. His latest book is "More Memories of the Old Geezer."

GUEST COLUMN: The singing ghost down by the riverbank

By Lonie Adcock, Guest Columnist | Posted: Wednesday, September 17, 2014 6:30 am

I know that I have written quite a group of stories about ghosts. I am asked by a lot of people, "do you believe in ghosts?" I answer, "there are a lot of strange things that happen in this old world — some you can explain; some you cannot."

This happened on a Saturday night while I was still on the Police Department. Most Saturday nights the town is a-hopping. You run from one side of town to the other. Being the Watch Commander, you move from one side to the other side, to backup and to being there when a car needs a supervisor.

I was on East Second Avenue when one of my patrol cars checked out with two subjects on East First Avenue.

I went to assist as fast as possible. When I got there and got out with the other unit I saw that it was two of our regular old drunks.

Lonie Adcock

Lonie Adcock of Rome is a retired Rome Police Department lieutenant. His latest book, "More Memories of the Old Geezer," is now available.

The officer came over to me. "Lieutenant," he said. "I don't know what they have been drinking but they keep babbling about a singing ghost." I remember laughing and saying "With what they drink, they are liable to see anything."

I walked over to them and spoke to the one named Walter. I asked "What's this about a singing ghost?" Walter pointed toward the railroad trestle. "There, down by the trestle. We heard it." "You heard what?" I asked. Then both of them blurted it out at the same time: "A singing ghost." I motioned for the officer to take them to the station and book them.

I watched as the police car turned onto Broad Street and then got in to my patrol car and started to the railroad trestle to see if I could hear the singing ghost. I stopped beside a small metal building that sat on the side of the railroad tracks. I could not get my car in any closer so I got out, picked up my flashlight and walked over to the edge of the trestle. I turned off my flashlight and stood still, listening for the singing ghost.

The night was quiet and being that close to the river gave me an eerie feeling. I listened but heard nothing. My walkie-talkie was having a fit. It never got quiet and I knew that it was only a matter of minutes until Radio gave me a call.

I turned to go back to my patrol car when I heard it. I shined my light over the bank but could not see anything. I could see the river and hear it, for there had been a lot of rain recently. I moved the light across what looked like, in the dark, a bunch of large vines growing on the bank. I got as close to the edge of the bank as I could and shined my light over the vines. I could see nothing.

The walkie-talkie got quiet and I stood still, listening. Then from the vines on the bank came a laugh. It said something that sounded like, "I showed them." Then it started in to sing.

That was too much. I moved close to the edge of the bank and played my flashlight over the vines. I could see nothing in the light but vines. It looked like they ran from the ground up and into the tree. I looked the ground over and found it was full of muscadines.

Vines were everywhere, but who was singing? Then Radio came on, giving me a backup call to one of the cars. I turned to go and the singing started back. As I got in my car I remember saying "Keep singing and I will be back."

It was one of the Saturday nights when all the natives got drunk and wanted to fight. All night long we booked them in, until we had no space left in the cells and we locked the door to the hallway in back of the cells and used it to hold them.

At the end of the shift I was so tired and ready for bed. But I had no intentions of going home and going to bed. The singing ghost was waiting for me.

I started down the hallway when one of the day shift policemen came down the hall. I stopped and talked to him a few minutes, telling him about the singing ghost. I could see that I had his attention. He told me he would come down to the trestle with me.

I pulled up beside the metal building with the patrol car. I got out and started to the trestle. It was good daylight now and you could see without a light. I walked over to where I had last heard the singing. I looked down the bank toward the river. The other officer was looking along the bank also. We could see nothing but vines running all over the place.

Then as if in answer to our thoughts, the singing started.

I moved over as close as I could get and looked down toward the river though the thick growth of vines. I could see the river at the bottom of the vines. I moved over to where the other officer was and looked at him. "Well," I asked. "What do you think?" He shrugged his shoulders, shaking his head.

We were standing talking when the singing started up again. It came in loud and clear.

A smile came on my face, for I had heard the song when I was growing up. Then I saw a place in the vines that looked like someone or something had crawled under them. I bent down to where I could see though the vines. There, wrapped up among the vines, was our singing ghost. We both started to laugh, for our singing ghost was one of our old drunks.

How to get him out of the vines was the question. If he moved and got loose, it was a good 20 feet to the water in the river. As I said earlier, the water was up and very swift. In his shape he wouldn't have a chance. I told the officer to call Radio and tell them what he had and let the Fire Department know.

We stood watching, hoping that he would be still until the Fire Department got there.

It wasn't too long before two firemen in a pickup pulled in. We showed them what we had. We talked for a few minutes and they got out some rope with harness and began to set up. They tied the ropes around the rails and began to move down though the vines to where he was.

I held my breath as they moved over to him. One fireman checked him out. Then, holding his nose, he said "OK, but very polluted."

I watched as they put the harness around him. The other officer and I pulled the slack out of the rope as they brought him up. We laid him on the ground and I told the fireman what a good job they had done.

I left it in the hands of the officer, and I headed for my car and bed.

That was one day that nobody had to tell me to go to bed. I slept most of the day, but that night found me headed back to the police station. On my way back to the station I got to thinking about the singing ghost. When they had brought up the fellow from the vines I could hardly believe my eyes.

The singing ghost was known by all the police as Pee Duckie. He was about 5-foot-6 and weighed about 100 pounds.

Lonie Adcock of Rome is a retired Rome Police Department lieutenant. His latest book is "More Memories of the Old Geezer."

GUEST COLUMN: Ghosts - Are they fact or fiction?

By Lonie Adcock, Guest Columnist | Posted: Tuesday, September 30, 2014 6:30 am

I've had several stories in the paper about ghosts. I met people who had read them and one of the questions I asked was "Do you believe in ghosts?" I had some who said they did, and some who said they didn't. I find more people that believe in them than those who don't.

One person who asked me stated that he did not believe in ghosts. He did not believe that there were cemetery lights. He said that he had worked around cemeteries and had never seen any lights. I had another man come up to me and we had quite a lengthy conversation about his experience with ghosts.

A lady came up to me and looked at me in a odd sort of way. "Are you psychic?" she asked. I answered "No, I don't think so. Why do you ask?" We got into a conversation about people who could see, feel and hear things that others couldn't. She stated that she could see things that others could not. She said that she was a psychic. I don't claim to be a psychic. If what you see on television and in movies makes a psychic then I know that I am not.

Lonie Adcock

Lonie Adcock of Rome is a retired Rome Police Department lieutenant. His latest book, "More Memories of the Old Geezer," is now available.

I talked to people who say they can see, hear and feel things that others can't. They describe it as a feeling that comes over them at times. When they get this feeling it sends cold chills down their backs and goose pimples on their arms. I was told that the hair stands up on the back of their necks. One man told me that when this happens he knows a spirit is near.

I believe that there are things in life that we do not understand. I believe that there are some people who can feel, see and hear things that others can't. A woman in Germany explained to me that they call this a person with sensitive feelings. There is a difference, in my opinion, between sensitive feeling and being psychic.

When I was a teen I had a couples of buddies that I used to go ghost-hunting with. We would load up a car with girls and off we would go. Now in those days, I went to just about every place in and around Floyd County that was supposed to be haunted. I am sure we missed some places, but not many.

I remember an incident that happened that I have wondered about down through the years.

I was working in construction at the time. We were remodeling the Esserman's clothing store on Broad Street. We had the roof tore off and were working twelve hours a day. It was on a Saturday that we got the roof back on and the concrete finisher moved in. I walked out on the street to find Duke and Carlton waiting for me.

I got in the car and sat down. Carlton immediately began to tell me that the girls were waiting for us. They had a place that was haunted that we hadn't been to. I listened but it didn't seem like too good of an idea for I had worked over sixty hours that week. I was tired. All I wanted to do was go home, take a bath, eat supper and go to bed.

Duke pulled in to the Callahan Street Park instead of taking me straight home. The girls were waiting for us. I told them that I was tired and didn't think that I could make it. They began to talk about this new place and looked at me with their big eyes. Finally I said I would go after I went home, took a bath, and had supper.

A short while later found me jammed like a sardine in the back seat of the car. We went though Cave Spring, headed for Alabama. I have no idea where we went for I must have gone to sleep. I woke up being shaken by one of the girls.

We were in a cemetery that had a small, white, wooden church next to it. I got out and one of the girls led the way to where the ghost was supposed to be. We all gathered around an old tombstone. It was six feet tall or more. A long tombstone about four feet high was at the foot. We stood with our back to the foot. Everyone was quiet. The only sound was the sound of crickets.

Then we heard a thump and a loud yell. I turned to find Carlton missing. I went around behind the tombstone to find him lying on his back on the ground. He let out a moan as if he was dying. I bent over and could see that his eyes were open. "Hey," I said, shaking him to get up. He sat up, letting out another moan. "What happened to you?" I asked. He got to his feet and looked around as if there was something there to be afraid of. He never said a word. Turning around, he went to the car and got in. I watched as he closed the door.

I looked around and could see that everyone was ready to leave.

As we usually did on a Saturday night after a ghost hunt, we went to Roy's for a coke. Carlton had come all the way back from over in Alabama not saying a word. With our cokes and fries we began to talk about what had happened. I looked at Carlton. "Come on, tell us what happened." He started out by saying, "You will not believe me if I tell you." "Try us," I said. He began to talk.

I listened as he told us how something had gone through him, lifting him up and over the four-foot tombstone. He said his body was in the air as he passed over the tombstone. I looked around at the girls and, with no more light than what we had, could see smiles on their faces. No one said anything and Carlton was quiet the rest of the time we were together.

We dropped Carlton off at his house and when he got out I heard someone giggle. "Girls," I said. "Be nice. Carlton had a shock tonight." We talked about what had happened later on.

We had another incident that took place on Park Road.

The girls wanted to go to Park Road and see if that place was haunted. We loaded up and away we went. Park Road ran from Black's Bluff Road to what was Highway 27 at that time. The road came out at the back of Darlington school close to McHenry School. A small dirt road ran up the hill to a level place surrounded by a group of oak trees. You had room to turn around once you got to the top.

We got out of the car and walked around to see if we could locate anything. I gave up and walked over and sat down on the fender of the car. Several of the girls and Carlton had come over and we were talking. One of the girls that was still looking let out a scream. I jumped off the car fender and went running over to where she was. "There," she said, pointing.

I looked and there on the ground lay Duke. I went over to him. He was out cold. I began to work with him and finally he moaned. I looked at Carlton and asked, "Can you drive?" "No license," he said. I didn't have a drivers license either at that time. I kept on working with him and finally got him to his feet. I helped him over to the car and got a towel out of the car for him to wipe his face. He had a scratch over his eyes with a big bruise. He had took a hard lick to make that kind of knot with a bruise.

He finally got all right and we drove back to the park to let the girls out. After dropping off Carlton we went to Duke's house. There he cleaned up the bruise and we sat down on the front porch to talk. I let him tell what had happened.

He told me that he had started to come over to the car where I was standing. Hearing a noise, which he thought was one of the girls, he turned. What happened next he had no idea. He came to when I was working on him. I left him wondering what had happened.

I look back and still wonder.

Did Carlton step backward and trip over the tombstone? He said he was thrown over it. Did he trip or was he thrown? Did Duke run into a tree and knock himself out or did a ghost hit him?

Again I ask, do you believe in ghosts? The two incidents happened while I was present. I can't say what happened — were they accidents or was it a ghost? It shall remain forever a mystery.

Lonie Adcock of Rome is a retired Rome Police Department lieutenant. His latest book is "More Memories of the Old Geezer."

GUEST COLUMN: The story of Peppermint Sally

By Lonie Adcock, Guest Columnist | Posted: Wednesday, October 15, 2014 6:30 am

This story started way back in the forties. There may be a few people who still remember the times I write about. They opened a place for young people to go and enjoy themselves, called Teen Canteen, in a building behind the City Auditorium. I worked during the week, but when they opened the door on Saturday night, I was there.

The place was chaperoned by grownups, and you didn't have to worry about someone jumping you. I had always loved to watch people dance. I had never had the chance to learn. I would sit and watch the boys and girls dancing and wish that I could get out there with them.

There was one girl who was very popular and all the boys wanted to dance with her. She would dance with several then come over and sit on the bench with me. We talked like young people did back then. One night she said, "come dance with me." I would had given anything I had to have

Lonie Adcock

Lonie Adcock of Rome is a retired Rome Police Department lieutenant. His latest book, "More Memories of the Old Geezer," is now available.

been able to dance with her. I slowly shook my head saying "I don't know how." She took my hand and pulled me up from the bench. We moved over to a place where no one was and she began to show me how to do the two-step. I recall when I left there that night I thought I had really done something.

I went to the Teen Canteen and would get on the floor with her. I was not the best two-stepper but she didn't seem to mind. I got to noticing that several times during the night she would go outside. When we got back on the dance floor she would smell like peppermint. I remember thinking "what is she doing that she comes back in smelling like that?"

One night as she went outside, I followed her to see what she was doing. I watched as she ducked around the side of the building out of sight. I walked around to where I could see her. She stood there smoking a cigarette. I went back inside, not letting her know that I had seen her smoking.

Lonie Adcock of Rome is a retired Rome Police Department lieutenant. His latest book is "More Memories of the Old Geezer."

GUEST COLUMN: Shorty and his water kegs

By Lonie Adcock, Guest Columnist | Posted: Monday, November 3, 2014 6:30 am

I was watching the television and a baseball game was on. As a rule I do not watch ball games of any kind. I am not like some sports fan. Baseball to me is a very boring game. If I was going to watch a ball game it would be some high school basketball game. Now that is said go ahead and criticize me.

I had not meant to get any one upset but had intended to tell you of a period in my life when I enjoyed a good ballgame if it was played by local people.

I remember back when I first started on the police department and was put into the car with the Whizz. On Sunday there would be local people playing baseball in the park at Hardy Avenue. Whizz and I would pull in and watch as much of the game as we could. Being on a Sunday, most of the time we would get to watch much of the game.

There was a man who rode a bicycle that had two small kegs mounted on the rear. Shorty, as he was

Lonie Adcock

Lonie Adcock of Rome is a retired Rome Police Department lieutenant. His latest book, "More Memories of the Old Geezer," is now available.

called, was a very small man. We often wondered how he rode the big bicycle with the two kegs on it. He would fill the kegs with ice and sell cold water at the ballgame.

Shorty would have to get up on something in order to get on the bicycle. His feet would barely touch the pedals. He would jump off the bicycle and run along beside it when getting off. Shorty would always give the Whizz and me a cold cup of water on a hot day.

Whizz drove the patrol car into the park one Sunday morning and got us parked in a spot where we could get out when necessary. We talked to some of the people who were gathering and found out that the Rome team was playing a team from Villa Rica. They began to arrive and started to do a little practice. The Rome team wore red pullovers. The team from Villa Rica wore blue.

This was a game like you did not see then — or now — even if you paid for it. This was a game where each team put everything they had into it.

The Whizz and I made a bet. We were big betters and we put our money into the ashtray where the winner could reach in and get it. We bet a coke on the game. Big money. Cokes were a nickel apiece back then.

That was one of those days when nothing was going on so we sat there and watched the game. About the middle of the game Shorty filled up two cups of cold water and brought it over to us. He talked to us a few minute until he saw a customer at his water kegs.

I remember that Shorty emptied his kegs several times that day. He would get on his bicycle and head up the road. It wouldn't be long before he was back with his keg full of water. He must have emptied his keg at least four times.

He came over to the car and, kidding, said, "you fellows want to escort me to the bank?" and showed us a sack full of change. Shorty was a good sport. Whizz reached in and got our dime out of the ashtray and said with a laugh, "keep an eye out so no one will rob me of my winnings."

On the corner of Hardy and Myrtle was a small store. In the summertime they would fill a big wooden barrel full of different soft drinks and pour ice over the top of them. When you reached in and got one, it was what we called back then iced cold.

That day, the Whizz pulled in front of the store and handed me the dime. "Since I am buying, you can go get them," he said. "No cakes or cookies," I asked, taking the dime. I went in and got the drinks and as I came out the door Shorty went by on his bicycle. He blew his horn at me. Shorty had a horn on his bicycle that sounded like a duck quacking.

The Whizz and I watched a lot of games on Hardy Avenue and at each game Shorty was there with his water kegs.

One day, the Whizz and I had just got into the patrol car and started to pull out from the station when we got the call. It was a Sunday morning and the weather was beginning to cool down. The dispatcher gave us a call that someone had hit a child on a bicycle at Myrtle and Pennington Avenue.

With lights and siren we got to the accident scene just as a ambulance arrived. We moved in and helped get the small body onto the stretcher. I remember looking at Whizz and shaking my head. The small body that we put on the stretcher was Shorty.

With the ambulance on the way to the emergency center, we began to do our report. We called for a pickup truck to come and carry the bicycle to the station. With the on-scene investigation over we started to the hospital emergency room. We entered the emergency room and a nurse who I will call Stella met us. She shook her head. "He died on the way in."

I looked at the Whizz, and I knew what he was feeling. Shorty had been a friend to the both of us.

We had told the driver of the car to go to the station and wait for us. We took the information at the emergency room and headed for the station. While the Whizz took the information and made the report, I went out back to look at the bicycle.

The car had hit the bicycle on the front wheels. This turned the bicycle around in the road, and the back end of the car again hit the front wheels. As if by some kind of miracle, the kegs had stayed attached to the back of the bicycle.

I walked over and turned on the spicket of one of the kegs. I stuck my finger in the water and smelled it. I then turned the other one on. I stuck my finger into a stream of something that had a light yellow look. I smelled my finger. It was not water. I smiled to myself and went inside.

I met the Whizz coming down the hall. "I need to look at the bike," he said. I walked back to the bike with him. I had believed that the chain had came off the brake and Shorty had run into the car, unable to stop. If he had tried to stop it with his legs they would not have been long enough to touch the ground.

Whizz and I agreed on what happened. The accident had been unavoidable.

I motioned for the Whizz to smell of the water in the keg. He stuck his finger under the fluid, then smelled it. A smile came on his face and he began to laugh. All the time that we knew Shorty he had been selling homemade brew.

He had water in one of the kegs and the brew in the other. He would give us a glass of water out of the water keg. He would give his customer the brew out of the other keg. He was a smart little fellow. We had a laugh out of it but never told anyone how Shorty had put one over on all of us.

Lonie Adcock of Rome is a retired Rome Police Department lieutenant. His latest book is "More Memories of the Old Geezer."

GUEST COLUMN: A few embarrassing incidents on patrol

BY Lonie Adcock, Guest Columnist | Posted: Wednesday, November 19, 2014 6:30 am

I am sure that there are those among us who have had their embarrassing moments. Maybe it is something you say or what you see. It could be that you do something foolish. In many ways we are capable of embarrassing moments through our actions. The ones that I am going to tell you about were beyond anything I could do to prevent them.

This incident happened at the forks of East Main and South Broad streets. We topped the hill on South Broad and saw two cars in the middle of the road, blocking the roads. I was riding with a partner by the name of Pete. All the old policemen knew Pete. A better partner you could not have. I would have gone anywhere with Pete as my back-up.

Pete was driving and as he brought the patrol car to a halt I jumped out. I heard the rip but paid no attention to it. As I exited the car a man in the crowd knocked a woman to the asphalt. He saw me as I came from the car and ran across the street going down Harper Avenue.

Lonie Adcock

Lonie Adcock of Rome is a retired Rome Police Department lieutenant. His latest book, "More Memories of the Old Geezer," is now available.

On the corner of Harper and East Main there was a house that had a high wall on the street side. The fellow I was chasing went over the wall, with me behind him. As I cleared the wall I heard the rip sound again. As I hit the ground I heard another rip sound — and a scream from the fellow that I landed on. How I did it I will never know, but I landed with my feet in his stomach. I never fell but stayed on my feet. I waited until he quit hollering and got him to his feet.

I put the handcuffs on him and walked him back up to where the others were. I got in the middle of the crowd and was listening to what had happened when Pete said, "the seat of your pants are ripped." I reached back and found that the pants leg was split and the only thing I had covering my back end was my Jockeys.

As I remember, I was standing in the middle of five young girls who could not hold their giggles. With the facts sorted out, I decided to get in the back seat and sit down with my prisoner. In those days there were no cages in the cars

I listened as the fellow told me his story.

He had been fishing with some buddies and came home early to find his wife out with some of her girlfriends. I asked him to justify hitting his wife and I would let him go. Oh, he gave a good reason for hitting his wife: She was supposed to stay at home while he was fishing. I asked him why did his wife have to stay at home while he was out having a good time.

I then told him what I thought about a man who beats on women. He got quiet for he saw that he was not going home.

We got into the station just as the shift was changing. When I got out of the car with my Jockeys showing, a cheer went up. I had no idea that anyone was in the station but the officers, so I pulled the legs of the pants up and put them down in my belt. Up the hall I went, to meet laughter from a group of people. I acted like everything was OK and waved as I turned the corner going to the locker room to change pants, but I was in no hurry to get back out with the crowd.

When I finally came out everything was quiet. Everyone was gone except the radio operator.

I remember another time when I had got a call to the emergency room at Floyd Hospital. I parked my patrol car and started inside. I opened the door and stepped inside the room. I turned the door loose and started to step when one foot went one way and the other foot the other. I was fighting to stay on my feet and not fall. Somehow I grabbed a hold of something on the wall that caused me to go across the room.

A woman was standing against the wall watching me. I reached out grabbed a doorknob and pulled myself toward her. Her eyes grew big as I reached out and hugged her to me. With both feet planted solid I looked the woman in the face. She smiled and said hello. I said hello, knowing that my face was red. She whispered, "I believe you can turn me loose now that you have quit dancing." I stood up releasing her and started to take a step.

I mumbled something to the effect or "I am sorry." As I turned, the same thing — one foot went north and the other foot went south. I slid, and, as the other officer said, I did the tootie fruity all over again. I remember the woman's eyes getting bigger as I headed for her. Safe again with my arms around a woman who I had never seen before. I was highly embarrassed.

Safe at last, I looked down into the eyes of the woman. She smiled and said, "We are going to have to quit meeting this way." With a red face, I moved along the wall to a chair. A nurse brought me a cloth and I took off my shoes and cleaned off the bottoms. I stood up to see if I could move without falling. On leaving I passed the woman still standing by the door. I went over and said, "I am sorry." She smiled and said, "any time you want to, just come on by."

I stopped at the door where I began my slipping. There on the floor was a wad of wax. You could see where I had stepped in the middle of it. I motioned for a nurse. I showed her the wax and said the next one to step in that may not be able to do the tootie fruity like me.

This next one is one of those incidents where everyone concerned is embarrassed. I remember that my partner was Pete, whom I worked with when there were two-men cars. Pete had a mischievous side as I did. We got along real well. I had a lot of laughs with Pete.

The call came to see a lady on Fourth Avenue because there was someone in her house. We pulled in at the address and were met by a lady. She said she came home from work and heard someone in her house. She opened the door and we went inside, guns drawn. The lady came in behind us and pointed toward a door. "In there," she whispered.

I moved over to the door to see if I could hear anyone. It was quiet. No noise of any kind came from the room. I motioned for Pete to open the door. Pete pushed the door open and I went through with gun in hand.

I got the surprise of my life. There, in the middle of the bed, were a man and a woman in their birthday suits. They sat up in bed and the woman let out a scream that almost busted my eardrums. I stood there with my gun pointed at them. Then, from behind me, I heard the lady speak. "Mother, what are you doing here in my house?"

I holstered my gun and turned to the lady who was standing with a look of disbelief on her face. I walked out of the room with Pete and asked the lady, "is that your mother and father?" "Mother yes, father no," she said. Pete and I told the lady we were leaving.

As we pulled away from the house I looked at Pete and we both started to laugh. What had happened was that Mama was doing a little hanky panky on the old man. She thought that they would be safe since the daughter was at work. In doing what they were doing they lost track of time.

We got a good laugh but, believe me, it was no fun going through a door to find the people inside with nothing on but their birthday suits.

Lonie Adcock of Rome is a retired Rome Police Department lieutenant. His latest book is "More Memories of the Old Geezer."

GUEST COLUMN: The two-hole outhouse

Posted: Tuesday, December 2, 2014 7:15 am

I was looking though Facebook and someone had put a picture of an outhouse on it. They had asked the question "does anyone know what this is?" Of course I did, it was an outhouse.

I knew because I was raised up back when there was one sitting out behind every house. They said "share if you have ever used one." I didn't share, but believe me when I say that I have used them. I have used them when the weather was hot and you held your breath while in it. I also used them when it was so cold that you tried to keep your shirt down over your bottom while the ice cold wind blew up though the hole.

There were all kind of outhouses back in those days. There were those that sat behind what we called the rich people's houses. They were fancy-made and looked like a child's playhouse. Only difference between a child's playhouse was the smell and, instead of furniture, there were one or two holes in a raised-up seat.

Lonie Adcock

Lonie Adcock of Rome is a retired Rome Police Department lieutenant. His latest book, "More Memories of the Old Geezer," is now available.

I had a friend in school who had one of those fancy outhouses. While playing with him one day I used the excuse to use the outhouse because I wanted to see inside of it. I stepped in and closed the door. This was on a hot day. There was no difference in the smell, but the inside looked like a rich man's house.

There were covers over the holes. This was the first outhouse that I had ever seen with two holes. There were windows on each side of it with curtains on them. I stood and looked in amazement. I looked around for paper but could not see a catalog anywhere. A roll of funny-looking paper was on a roll of some sort, hanging on the wall. I pulled off a piece of it and smelled of it. I will never forget the surprise that I got. It smelled like spice. It was the kind that you put in fried apple pies.

I pulled off a big piece and put it in my pocket. I remember asking my mother what it was and what did you do with it. Boy did I get a shock when she told me rich folks wiped their bottoms with it. I remember thinking I would stick with the catalog. Who wanted to walk around with their bottom smelling like apple pie?

Time went on and I got to where it was a chore to get up in the middle of a cold night, put on your clothes and go out to the outhouse. I think everybody will remember that most everyone had a potty that sat under the bed. You used it during the night, and in the morning you emptied it into the outhouse. Any way you looked at it, you had to hit the cold mornings. The potty was a household item for many a year. I have seen some mighty fancy ones sitting under beds. I once knew a woman who collected potties.

We moved to Reece Street in North Rome. I was working in construction at that time. A dream had come true; we had a two-hole outhouse.

They were rare in rental houses at that time. When we tore out lumber the man in charge of the construction would give the lumber to us. The man who drove the truck for the company lived two doors up from me. He would bring all the old used lumber and dump it off at my house. I began to rebuild our outhouse.

I began by putting a red tin roof on it. Even in the moonlight it stood out. A mixture of paint, which turned out to be a nice dark gray, put the finishing touch to the outside. I had neighbors who would walk by just to see what was next.

Off came the door, and a partition went between the holes. I had got some paneling and made the doors. I must admit that I had outdone myself, for the door looked like a million. I would look at it and smile to myself.

We were tearing out an office building when I got the toilets seats. Man, they were pretty and white. They went in and covered the holes. I put cardboard around the walls and then paneled them. It looked good. Into each side a holder was put to place the catalog in. Then I remembered the rolled paper that made your bottom smell like apple pie.

I went to the five-and-dime and bought me a package of it. I smiled all the way home. I got home and tore the paper open. What a disappointment. The paper did not smell like apple pie. It had an odor, but it smelled more like a perfume that the girls wore in those days. I believe that they called it spice. Oh what the heck, I thought, placing the spiced paper in the outhouse. A spice bottom would smell better than an old catalog.

I went into the dime store to buy a book and there on the counter were perfumed pots. You opened them and they would last for weeks. I grabbed two, paid for them and hurried home. My mother laughed at me when I placed them in the outhouse. That put the finishing touch on the outhouse.

One of my neighbors let curiosity get the best of her. She had been up the street to the store. She stopped and asked if she could use the outhouse. My mother said help herself. We waited for her to come back. I had began to think she wasn't coming back when the door opened. She came up to my mother and said, "All my life I have never seen an outhouse that was a pleasure to go in." She pointed to our outhouse, "That is, without a doubt, the finest one I have ever been in."

Word got out in the neighborhood and people came by to take a look. They would leave shaking their heads. Well, after all, back in those days how many outhouses could you go in, sit and read a paper in a perfumed room, and leave with a bottom that smelled like spice?

Lonie Adcock of Rome is a retired Rome Police Department lieutenant. His latest book is "More Memories of the Old Geezer."

GUEST COLUMN: Rich girl learns poor boy has a heart

Posted: Tuesday, January 20, 2015 7:15 am

Away back when most of you were not born there were The Rich and then there were The Poor. We never knew the people who had all the money. I met some of those that had a job and thought they were rich. Most of them did ride in cars where I had to walk or, if I had a nickel, ride the bus.

At the ripe old age of 13, I took a job washing dishes in order for my family to eat and have a place to live. Made a big old three dollars and a half working nine hours a day, six days a week.

By the time this story took place I was somewhere around 14 and working in construction. The pay was a little better. I had learned to do carpenter work, which was called third-degree. That meant I could drive a nail into a piece of wood without the union getting on me. The pay was somewhere around $25 dollars for a 40-hour week.

I was working with a full-time job but hadn't managed to have an automobile and wear fancy

Lonie Adcock

Lonie Adcock of Rome is a retired Rome Police Department lieutenant. His latest book, "More Memories of the Old Geezer," is now available.

clothes. I still fitted into the poor boy stage. My fancy clothes were a pullover shirt with turned up jeans. Oh yes, I had a maroon pair of Western boots with a fancy design. I wasn't rich, but I stood out among the other poor boys. Rolled up jeans with maroon boots — I can't imagine what I looked like if it was now.

The main source of entertainment was the movies. At that time we had the DeSoto, the Gordon and the one we called the rathole — the Rivoli. The Rivoli was the one that we went to most of the time, for it was the poor folks' movie. They showed the cliffhangers every weekend with good old Roy, Tex or Gene. We didn't think we were poor at that time; we thought, and knew, we had less than some others. The poor boys and girls had one thing going for them — a big heart.

What happened let me know that, poor or not, I was as good as anyone.

The movies were closed on Sunday, which left the boys and girls no place to go, but then the Rome News-Tribune let everyone know that the Lindale movie would open on Sundays at 1 p.m. for a matinee. My buddy Jimmy and I got to Lindale and got in place, in the middle of the bridge. The line to the auditorium went a good block long before the movie opened. We were all in line talking when I heard a remark about red boots.

I turned to see a girl walking around in circles, making fun of my boots and jeans. She was what we called a hoity toity poor little rich girl. She was really putting it on me, thick and heavy. I walked up to her and looked her over from head to toe. She did something then that burned me up — she bowed and said something to the effect of "bow and greet the well-dressed man of the hour." I clenched my fist and turned my back to her and went back to where Jimmy was.

Jimmy began telling me "pay no attention to her." He said "when you clenched your fist I thought you were going to hit her." "No," I said. "You don't hit girls ever, regardless of what they say." The line began to move and we made it inside.

It was every Sunday to the movie we would go. It was every Sunday that little Hoity Toity would look me up and start her act. I had told Jimmy if she was there and started on me this Sunday, it would be my last time to come.

She was there, sitting on the rail that was on the bridge. "Hey, Red Boots Boy, how long did it take you to shine them this time?" I turned to look at her and she let out a scream and jumped down off the rail. Everyone moved back, wondering what had happened. Everyone was looking at me for they knew that I had done nothing to her. She was jumping up and down, screaming at the top of her lungs.

I took a look at her and saw what had happened. She had sat down on an ant bed. It was a big red ant bed. They were all over her. They had got on her face. All us old jean-wearers usually had a big red handkerchief in our back pockets. I grabbed mine and began to wipe the ants off of her.

I remember taking the handkerchief and wiping them off her back and legs. She was wearing a dress. In those days you didn't pull up little girls' dresses. I thought about what I was doing and the trouble it could get me in. I got her wiped off as much as possible and then grabbed her and ran to the front of the auditorium. I told the lady what had happened and they took her into a back room. In a few minutes, her mother and father arrived and took her to the hospital.

On the way back home that night Jimmy gave me something to think about. He said I had pulled her dress up above her head. That scared me. I worked all the next week thinking about what they would do to me for what I had done.

Come Sunday, Jimmy and I went back to the Movie at Lindale. I was about in the middle of the bridge, standing and talking, when this big old Buick pulled up and stopped. A lady spoke and motioned for me to come to the car. I must have looked scared for she said, "Would you come up to the front of the auditorium and talk to us?" I said "yes ma'am" and then I notice Hoity Toity sitting in the back seat.

I walked over to Jimmy and told him who it was and they wanted to see me up at the front of the auditorium. I imagined all kind of things on my way. I walked in through the door and came face to face with a policeman. I must have looked scared out of my wits for the policeman said "Easy, man. Everything is OK." When he said that it helped some.

He introduced me to the mother and father of little Hoity Toity. The old man stuck out his hand and I took it. He told me how much he appreciated what I had done for his daughter. He said that if I had not rubbed her down wiping the ants off she would probably have died. She had stayed in the hospital several days, taking shots.

Her mother then came over and, taking my hand, asked if I would be — I believe she said "Rhonda's" — guest and sit with her in the movies. She said, "After all, the stuff she said and done was to get you to notice her." I looked at Jimmy and she spoke up, saying "he can be her guest too." You better believe I would be her guest, for that would save me a quarter.

I sat down beside her and the movie started. I could tell that she was very uncomfortable. I took her hand and got up. She followed me to the front lobby. I motioned for her to sit down. I began to tell her that everything was all right. Big old tears began to roll down her cheeks. She said "I have treated you awfully mean." I assured her that it was OK, but to always remember that us poor boys have hearts too. To hurt someone's feelings is easy; it is hard to take back.

The movie was over and I got up to leave when Jimmy came over to me. She said "wait." I walked back over to her and she handed me my big red handkerchief. I took it, folding it and putting it in my back pocket. I smiled and turned to walk away, saying "us poor boys have a heart too." Then came a whisper: "I washed it myself, just for you." I waved and moved out though the door.

I don't recall ever seeing her again. I hope those little red ants learned her a lesson. Sticks and stones can break bones that will heal but words can harm you for the rest of your life.

I worked all week worried about what was going to happen. That proved to me never to worry about what is going to happen. Prepare yourself and face the music. My experience didn't turn out too bad. I had a clean handkerchief washed by the hands of little Hoity Toity for a poor boy and a reward of 25 cents, no popcorn.

Lonie Adcock of Rome is a retired Rome Police Department lieutenant. His latest book is "More Memories of the Old Geezer."

GUEST COLUMN: The wolf-man on Cotton Avenue

Posted: Wednesday, February 25, 2015 6:00 am

I am sure that most people have seen or heard about the old movie "The Wolf Man." It was about a man who turned into a wolf on a full moon. He would run the countryside, howling and attacking people. He could only be killed with a silver bullet. Later a movie was made about a werewolf that stood upright on two feet but had a head like a wolf.

This was all pure fiction. I have never seen anything that would make me believe such a critter ever existed. A critter that ran upright and had the head of a wolf would have a hard time attacking me. He would have to be fast on his feet.

I was investigating a big bird on Cotton Avenue. I was talking to the lady who the big bird got after, when an old gentleman started to talk about a wolf-man that lived on the river. I didn't think much about it at the time, for I had a big bird that attacked the lady. We caught the big bird — which was an ostrich — and that made the call complete.

Lonie Adcock

Lonie Adcock of Rome is a retired Rome Police Department lieutenant. His latest book, "More Memories of the Old Geezer," is now available.

I worked a few more days and then went to the third shift. Everything was quiet until I got a letter from the front office instructing me to keep a good check on Cotton Avenue. People had called saying their animals were missing. Chickens were being taken from their pens and eaten. I remember thinking, "What else is going to happen on Cotton Avenue?"

After it got quiet, I went down to Cotton Avenue to see if there was anything going on. It was a bright, moonlit night. I turned off my headlights with my window down to see if I could see anything. I was easing along when I heard a voice say, "Hey, Police." I stopped the car and looked around, trying to see where the voice had come from. There on the porch where the old gentleman had talked about the wolf-man sat someone. I stopped the car and walked over to where he was.

He began to talk before I got to him. "He is back," he said. "Who is back?" I asked. I had forgotten about the wolf-man, but he began to talk and it went something like this:

"I am talking about the man who is half man and half wolf. He lives on the river. In certain times of the year he comes close to the houses. He has been coming back for the last two weeks. I come out at night to cool off and smoke a cigarette. I sit here quietly and listen. When he gets close to the house I go inside."

He stopped and I asked, "Have you seen this wolf-man?" "Sure enough have," he answered. I could not believe what the old gentleman was saying, but in my business you had to ask questions. As close as I can remember, this is what he said:

"He is about five feet tall 'cause he runs bent over. He has long hair all over him. His teeth is long, with fangs. He is close to us now. I am going inside. Be careful, officer, for he is dangerous."

I watched him as he closed the door behind him. I remember saying to myself with a smile on my face, "Sure he is dangerous." Then I reached for the door handle and froze. A sound the likes of which I had never heard came from down toward the river. It was a sound between the screaming of a high-pitched voice and a growl.

I got in the car and called for another car to come to me. I had then, and still do have, a sawed off shotgun. I used to put the shotgun down between the seats when I got in the car. I now placed the shotgun in the seat beside me. I eased on toward the river where the sound had come from.

The night was quiet, and with the window down I could hear the wind blowing in the trees. But when I stopped the car and got out, I realized it was not the wind. There was a small lake and woods beside the road. I reached and got the shotgun.

As I got out of the car I was met with another loud scream and then a growl. It came from a tree close to me. I reached back though the door and got my flashlight. I waited, then from in front of me — a growl. It sounded like a dog. I had the shotgun loaded with double aught buckshot. I had no idea what it was. A high-pitched scream, and then something was running in the grass and weeds in front of me. Then what sounded like a growl came from the tree again.

I could see the lights from the other police car as it turned onto Cotton Avenue. I took my flashlight and signaled for him to come in with his lights off. He pulled up behind my car and got out. I motioned for him to be quiet. He came over to me and I explained to him what the old man had said and what I had heard. He laughed, saying, "Lieutenant, you don't believe that do you?" Before I could answer the loud scream came from just a few feet in front of us.

I turned the shotgun in the direction of the sound. Then one of the most gruesome growls that I have ever heard came from the tree. I looked over at the officer and he had his gun in his hand. "Did you hear that?" I asked. He shook his head, never taking his eyes from the bushes. I moved around in front of the car. "Ready?" I asked. He laid his gun on the hood of the car and shook his head.

I moved, making a noise with my feet, and whatever was in the bushes let out a low growl. The bushes shook a few feet in front of me. The sound of the shotgun in the still of the night sounded like a cannon. A sound that I will never forget came from where I had shot. It let out a scream that sounded like a woman. I remember thinking that I had shot someone who was playing a joke on me. Silently I kept my gun pointed toward the last sound. Nothing. Then from down on the riverbank, a loud scream. And everything got quiet.

The officer came around the car to me. "Lieutenant, you hit something. I saw it run out though the bushes." I remember laughing and saying "If it had not been a shotgun I would not have hit it." My hands at the time of the last scream were not too steady. I want someone to tell me that they have never been scared. Being scared and being a coward are two different things. You can be scared and still stand up and face whatever it is. A coward turns tail and runs.

We stood around for a while but everything was quiet. We talked about it and came to the conclusion that, whatever it was, there were two of them.

The dispatcher called the car telling him to investigate a gunshot close to the river off of Cotton Avenue. I assured dispatch that we were there and had control of the situation. We decided that, whatever it was, we would have no more trouble that night. The dispatcher came over to me when we were getting off and asked "did you hit what you shot at?"

I motioned toward the officer who had been with me. "Ask him."

I went back, sat down, and started doing reports. I could hear the men ragging the officer out in the hallway. Then the door opened and the officer came in. "Come in here and laugh at the Lieutenant and tell him he is crazy," he said. He got no takers so he closed the door.

I sat many nights with the window down and my shotgun resting in the seat beside me, waiting for the wolf-man. We never got any more calls. I have often wondered what it was. As far back as I can remember, I have heard of black panthers that roamed this area. I have never seen one. I have seen bears, but no wolf-man or black panthers.

I will say, though, that if you are close when whatever it is lets out a scream or a low growl, chill-bumps will run your backbone.

Lonie Adcock of Rome is a retired Rome Police Department lieutenant. His latest book is "More Memories of the Old Geezer."

Sponsored From Around the Web

GUEST COLUMN: An old case - Pookey and the fires

By Lonie Adcock, Guest Columnist | Posted: Wednesday, March 18, 2015 6:30 am

This may not seem to you to be a subject to write about. I remember it with a smile on my face. I would never harm an animal any way, but sometimes you have to do things to prevent other things from happening.

Back when I was working plainclothes as an investigator with the city of Rome Police Department, a series of fires began to break out. I got with the fire department and they said the fires had been set. A case of arson.

I talked to the fire marshal and decided to see if I could help him out. When the fire department would get a call, I would go and walk around among the spectators. I was looking for a face that showed up at all the fires.

The first one that I went to was on East Second Avenue. I walked around in the crowd, taking in all the faces of the spectators. I was watching one young boy when something grabbed me by the cuff of my pants. It let out a yelp and started to back up with my pants leg in its mouth.

Lonie Adcock

Lonie Adcock of Rome is a retired Rome Police Department lieutenant. His latest book, "More Memories of the Old Geezer," is now available.

I reached down and grabbed it by the back of the head, shaking it loose from my pants leg. It was having a fit and this lady came up. She began to yell, "Pookey! Pookey! What have you done?" I handed the small dog to her. She gave me a hard look saying, "Pookey, did the mean old man hurt you?"

The fire was put out and everyone left. I got in my car and went back to headquarters.

The radio operator informed me that another fire was reported in the same area where the other fire had been. I parked my car a distance away and walked in. A crowd had gathered and I walked around among them.

I saw in the crowd the same young man that had been to the other fire. I backed up, watching him. I was so intent on watching him that I didn't see Pookey until he had grabbed the cuff on my pants and began to run backward. He almost pulled my leg from under me.

I reached down and got him by the head to where he could not bite me. I looked for the woman who had got him before. She saw me holding Pookey by the head and came running. "Pookey! Oh Pookey, is he hurting you?" She grabbed him and said, "if you grab Pookey that way again, I will call the police to you."

She turned and I walked over to the young fellow watching the fire. I struck up a conversation with him. I talked to him a few minutes and knew I had found the person who was starting the fires. I didn't have enough to arrest him, but I found out where he lived.

I had found out that the young man was from Chattanooga, Tennessee. I called the police department there and talked to one of their detectives. He was proud to hear that I had found him because they had a case of arson against him. That gave me enough to pick him up.

Then I was informed by the radio operator that another fire had been called in from East First Avenue.

I opened up my desk drawer and took out a can of mace. It was issued to us to spray dogs. It didn't hurt them but they would leave you alone.

Prepared for Pookey, I went to the scene of the fire. I parked as close to the fire as possible. I walked in and, sure enough, here come Pookey and he grabbed the cuff on my pants. I took the mace and sprayed him good.

He backed up and here came the woman and grabbed him up in her arms. The mace from Pookey hit her in the face. She took out a handkerchief and wiped her eyes. "Oh Pookey, what have you got into?" she asked. She then pointed her finger at me and said "I still may call the police to you for the way you handled Pookey."

I ignored her and walked over to the young fellow and placed him under arrest.

With the arrest of the young fellow, the fires were no longer set. It got quiet. I would be driving down East Second Avenue and see the lady and Pookey walking, but I never ran across them at a fire scene again.

Lonie Adcock of Rome is a retired Rome Police Department lieutenant. His latest book is "More Memories of the Old Geezer."

GUEST COLUMN: Walking the log

Posted: Wednesday, April 1, 2015 6:15 am

I stood still, looking at the tree laying across the creek. It was about three feet above the water. I remember a cousin that was with me said, "Come on, you can walk the log."

I have had a slight fear of high places ever since I was a kid. I have worked at construction, climbed ladders and walked steel that was put in the top of buildings, and I still have a fear of high places. But I said a fear, not that I wouldn't climb with the best of them.

Let's go back and see what got me into this situation at the log. Where the post office is now, there used to be a forest with a small creek running through it. It ran into the river, down where the railroad trestle is. We would hunt hickory nuts in the woods there. This time Junior, a cousin of mine, had talked my mother into letting me go fishing with him.

Lonie Adcock

Lonie Adcock of Rome is a retired Rome Police Department lieutenant. His latest book, "More Memories of the Old Geezer," is now available.

I was five years younger than Junior. He would come and get me and take me fishing. With poles ready, we followed the creek down though the woods to where it went into the river. There was a big tree that had fallen across the creek and Junior used to walk across it to what looked like a good place on the river bank. I had been across this tree many times before.

The water had been up and there were deep holes of water in the creek. We had fished in all the holes. Not catching anything, Junior decided that we would go to the mouth of the creek where it went into the river. When we came to the place where the tree lay across the creek, Junior went first to make sure that the tree would hold our weight.

I remember him saying, "Come on, Lonie. It will not break." I stood still, not saying anything. Just shaking my head. Junior put down his fishing pole and came back to me. "What is the matter? You have walked that tree before." I finally got one word out of my mouth. "Snake." I remember that Junior had a fear of snakes. He wasn't by himself. I had then a dislike for snakes. Still do. If they will leave me alone, I will not bother them.

Junior looked to where I had pointed. There, on a limb that he had held onto to cross the creek, was a big snake. This was a huge snake. It looked to be a good six feet long. It lay to where, when Junior had held onto the limb, he had his hand within a few inches of its head.

I heard a funny sound and turned to see Junior fall to the ground. I went over to him. He lay there with a odd look on his face, as white as a sheet. I sat down beside him, not realizing that he had fainted.

I started to talk to him, telling him why I didn't cross the tree to him. He lay still, so I quit talking. I must have sat there a good 10 minutes before he made a sound. He sat up and, looking real funny, jumped to his feet. He looked at me and made me promise not to tell anyone what had happened. As small as I was, I didn't know what had happened. He had fainted, but that didn't mean anything to me. I thought he had got tired and lay down to rest.

As we stood there Junior realized we had a problem. He had put our rods and reels, along with the bait, on the end of the tree. I looked at the snake and knew that I was not going to get them as long as the snake was on the tree limb. I looked at Junior, shaking my head, We sat down on the ground and watched the snake. He was sunning himself and didn't seem to be in any hurry to leave. "What are we going to do?" I asked. Junior shook his head. "Don't know."

The rods and reels belonged to Junior, and if it had been up to me we would leave them there for the snake to fish with. I could see that Junior was not going to leave his fishing equipment there.

Junior sat looking at the snake on the tree limb. I got up and went up a trail that led to the railroad. Once on the track, I began a search for some rocks. Putting some in my pocket and carrying one in each hand, I went back to where Junior sat. Now I have always been good at hitting what I threw a rock at. As small as I was then, I had found that a rock can be a good weapon. Junior sat still staring at the snake. He seemed to be in a trance.

I moved in to what I thought was a good position and let go with a rock. The rock hit the snake in the head. He moved, raising his head up about a foot high off the tree. I let another rock go. Wham on the head again. This seem to irritate him. He rolled up into a ball with his head up and looking around. I had two more rocks left and I knew that I had to make them good.

I had picked up a rock that had a sharp edge to it. I walked in as close as I dared. His head was sticking up. I let go with the rock. Then, to my surprise, he rolled up into a ball and fell in to the water. He was rolling around in the water. I let go with the other rock. I hit him. But where, I have no idea. I watched as he rolled and moved around in the creek. He went out into the river.

I watched as he went out of sight. I looked at Junior. He was still as white as a piece of cotton. I ran across the log and picked up the rods and reels along with the bait. Junior looked at me and said, "I think I have had enough fishing for one day." Picking up the rods and reels, pouring out the bait, we headed up to the railroad tracks. Neither one of us had any desire to meet up with another snake that day.

Junior and I went fishing a lot more times after that. I do remember that we never went fishing in a place that was grown up to where you could not see where you put your feet. I did not know until later years what kind of effect that a fear of something can have on you.

Lonie Adcock of Rome is a retired Rome Police Department lieutenant. His latest book is "More Memories of the Old Geezer."

GUEST COLUMN: Eyes in the back of the head

Posted: Wednesday, April 15, 2015 6:15 am

All my life I have heard that mothers have eyes in the back of their heads. We all know that is impossible. I have looked at the backs of people's heads all my life, hunting those eyes. Now, at my age, you would think that I would give up. I am not giving up, for some day one will slip up and I will see her eyes looking at me from the back of her head.

Let me give you several examples for believing that women have eyes in the back of their heads.

I was a little tot when I came in from the outside to smell tea cakes cooking. Some people may not know what tea cakes are. Back when I was growing up, that was one of the goodies that my mother would cook.

I remember slipping in the kitchen as quiet as a mouse. My mother's back was turned to me. I walked over to the pan of tea cakes and stood still, watching my mother's back. She acted as if I

Lonie Adcock

Lonie Adcock of Rome is a retired Rome Police Department lieutenant. His latest book, "More Memories of the Old Geezer," is now available.

wasn't there. I reached out to take one of the tea cakes from the plate. "Young man, don't you dare put your hand anywhere around that plate." I drew my hand back and eased from the room. She never looked at me. I always wondered how she had known I was there.

Another time, it was my birthday. It had been a long morning since breakfast. I could smell fried chicken and an odor of something else cooking. I had no idea what smelled so good.

Now us kids stayed out of the kitchen when our mother was cooking. I eased to the door to see my mother at the other end with her back to me. There was a platter of fried chicken sitting on the table. Next to it was what smelled so good — a banana pudding. I watched my mother's back. She never let on that she knew that I was there. I slipped into the kitchen and reached for a piece of the chicken. Then, never turning to look at me, "Touch that chicken and you will get the seat of your pants dusted." I drew my hand back from the chicken wondering how she did that. She saw me but never looked at me.

It really got next to me. I was small, but still I wondered how she had seen me without turning her head. With a stomach full of fried chicken and banana pudding I wanted to find out so I asked her how she had done it. I looked at her for an answer but my sister spoke up, "You didn't know Mama had eyes in the back of her head? She can see you without turning her head."

I couldn't believe that, so I got up and went over and looked at the back of my mother's head. I couldn't see any eyes. I sat back down and asked, "If you have eyes in the back of your head, how do you hide them from us?" I got that all-knowing look. From then on, I would walk around behind my mother trying to see her eyes in the back of her head. No matter how hard I tried, she managed to keep them hid from me.

It's not only mothers who have eyes in the back of their heads. It's women in general.

Do you men remember when you were young, a pretty girl would walk by and you followed them with your eyes? Your wife never looked up, but made a statement something like, "Put your eyes back in your head. You can only look at the menu, not order from it." How did she see the pretty girl that you were looking at? She had never turned her head and the girl was over across the room, behind her. There is the proof; all women have eyes in the back of their heads.

It's a beautiful Sunday and you have the family out riding around. Take them to the park and, later, to a nice place to eat. You have a stomach full of good food and enjoyed a family get-together, then you start home. You pull up to the intersection and look both ways. Nothing coming. You start to pull out and your wife shouts at you, "Watch out!" You hit the brakes and a car comes from out of nowhere, barely missing you. How did she see that car? It came from behind you. There again proves what I have been saying: Women have eyes in the back of their heads.

Your wife says something to you. You turn your back to her and stick out your tongue. "I saw that," she says. How did she see when her back was to you? You were back to back and she saw you stick out your tongue. Impossible, you say, but it happens.

This is the one that gets me.

You are relaxed in your easy chair. In comes your wife, saying "get out of that chair and take out the garbage." She proceeds into the next room. You make a face at her back. She is already in the room but says, "I saw that." Impossible. There was a wall between you. You get up and go in the kitchen and start to get the garbage. As you leave the room you mumble something. "I heard that," she shouts at you. You think, "Can't I ever win? Now she is hearing things that I am thinking."

I have never really believed that women have eyes in the back of their heads, but I can't help looking — hoping to see them peeping at me. If you are ever close to me and I jump up and start pointing and shouting "There it is," you will know that at last I have seen the eyes in the back of a woman's head.

Lonie Adcock of Rome is a retired Rome Police Department lieutenant. His latest book is "More Memories of the Old Geezer."

GUEST COLUMN: The Colonel, his books and his stories

Posted: Wednesday, April 29, 2015 6:15 am

My father passed away when I was 11 years old. I grew up without the influence of a father. My mother did a good job bringing up three boys after he passed away. When I look back at people who had an influence on my life, I know one man's name as good as I know mine. I will call him Colonel. That is what he wanted me to call him, and that is who he has been for many a year.

It was in the early 1940s and we lived in North Rome on Reece Street. I was at that time working with a construction firm. We built everything from big department stores to outhouses. If it was a job in construction, our construction firm would take it on.

Lonie Adcock

Lonie Adcock of Rome is a retired Rome Police Department lieutenant. His latest book, "More Memories of the Old Geezer," is now available.

I would leave home in the morning and walk to the office of the outfit that I worked for. I went to work at 8 a.m. so I would have to leave around about 7 o'clock. There was not the pawn shop on North Broad at that time, there were houses. I have always been a reader. I noticed that there were, in front of this one house, books for the garbage man to pick up.

I wanted those books but only had time to get to work. I didn't dare to stop for I would have been late. It broke my heart to leave those books laying there to be hauled away as trash. I believe then as I do now, a good book is not trash. A book should be passed on to someone who will enjoy it, not thrown in the trash dump.

I racked my brain trying to figure out a way to get those books. It came to me that the only way was to talk to the man who was throwing them away. It was on Saturday morning that I got up the nerve to go up and talk to him.

As I approached his house I saw him sitting on the porch. I walked up to the lower step and said "Good morning, sir." His face lit up with a big smile. "Why good morning," he replied. "Sir," I said. "I would like to talk to you for a few minutes if you don't mind." I noticed that when I said "sir" his face would light up with a smile. He said, "Come on up, young man, and tell me what's on your mind."

I went up and sat down in a chair and turned to him. I explained to him that I had seen books thrown in the garbage and wondered if there was any way that I might get them. I explained to him that I worked and would try to pay him for them. He listened, never changing his facial expression. When I was through, I remember thinking I had struck out with him.

He smiled and I thought this is it. "Let me say this is the most admirable thing that I have ever heard," he said. "You could have picked them up and carried them with you. Instead you came to me and asked me for them. You, son, have been raised right." I remember he talked on and I listened. I was getting a little nervous for he had not said yes or no. Then he smiled and got up, saying he would be back.

He came back in a few minutes and handed me a stack of books. He then went back in and came back with two Coca-Colas. He removed the tops and handed me one. I sat there and we talked about the kind of books that we liked. I found out he was a western story reader.

We became good friends. I would go up on Saturdays when I didn't have to work and sit and talk with him. He always had a cold drink and a piece of cake handy. I found out that he had been in the Army. He had held the rank of colonel. Several times he pulled out a box of pictures and we looked at them.

He had been in the Pacific with General MacArthur. Now he had what he called a walking cane that he used to help him walk. He had got shot in the knee. His knee would not bend when he walked. When he sat down he would have to take his hands and bend his knee.

He was a very Christian man. I found out that he was from Michigan. He had been sent to Battey General Hospital when he got shot. He went though the rehabilitation and discharged when he was well. He would laugh and say the weather in Michigan was not good for a knee like his, so he decided to live in Rome.

If I didn't have to work on Saturday, the morning was spent with the old Colonel. He had some stories about being in the Philippines that was as good as some in the books he gave me.

I had been working a lot on Saturdays and hadn't got to talk to the Colonel as much as I wanted to. I was off on this particular Saturday and when I got up I went to see him. His house was locked up and no one was anywhere to be seen. I went over to the house next door and asked them if they knew where the Colonel was. She wiped her eyes and said "You didn't know that the Colonel had a heart attack and died. They buried him last week."

I sat down on the steps and wiped the tears from my eyes. I knew that I had lost something more precious than anything in this world, a true friend.

I learned from the lady that the Colonel referred to me as his young friend. She said he talked about the time we spent talking about books and his time in the service. He had spent over 20 years in the Army. They had retired him because of his knee. He told me that he was a map maker. When they took an island from the Japanese he would map it for the Army.

You never knew that he had been wounded in service. If you asked him what was wrong with his knee, he would reply "I donated this knee so I could live in the greatest country in the world: The United States of America." The Colonel was a true American, a Christian and a kind and gentle man.

Lonie Adcock of Rome is a retired Rome Police Department lieutenant. His latest book is "More Memories of the Old Geezer."

GUEST COLUMN: Camping in the snow on our toes

Posted: Wednesday, May 13, 2015 6:15 am

Most men at one time or another have camped out. They set up their tents close to a trout stream and, early the next morning, they are off to the creek bank.

If it's a good day, they catch their limit, clean them and cook a feast on a small stove. Fish all cooked, they dig in. They eat until all is gone to find that they are still hungry. Then it's hop into the car and back to the hamburger joint they saw as they were coming in. The sleeping bag is not thick enough to make the ground soft. After a few days of this they've had enough so they pack up and go home.

Lonie Adcock

They tell their wives and co-workers what a good time they had, and all about the big trout they caught. Everyone believes them but their wives, who have seen them walking bent over from sleeping on the ground. They've already decided to get rid of the tent and to buy a camper or motor home.

Lonie Adcock of Rome is a retired Rome Police Department lieutenant. His latest book, "More Memories of the Old Geezer," is now available.

I have had an experience of sleeping on the ground in a small tent. The weather was cold and the snow came down, which didn't help matters much.

My outfit moved from Worms, Germany, to the mountains close to the Russian border. It didn't get much above zero during the day; at night it dropped below, and stayed that way. As the fellows who have been there know, you get half a tent. My tent buddy, bless his heart, had one of those noses that make a sound like someone sawing wood. A reliable source (my wife) says I sound like a laughing hyena when I sleep. I wouldn't know, for I have never stayed awake to find out. But I would wake up when my buddy was sawing that cord of wood, and get up to go sleep in the truck.

When we got to where we were going and set up camp, cold and tired, I had a cup of cold instant coffee with a can of beanie weenies for supper and went to sleep without any trouble. It was still dark when I woke up but I could see that some of the others were outside of their tents. I got up and joined them to see what was going on. Then came a whishing noise and what looked like a streak of fire in the sky over our heads.

This didn't set too good with me for I had never seen or heard anything like it.

They were lined up one behind the other. About the time one got out of sight another one would go over. Our company commander said, "Listen up. Everyone go back to sleep. It is only the Russians having fun." I remember that what I saw and heard didn't sound like fun.

I found out the next day that the Russians had a firing range where they fired artillery shells. The whishing sound and fire in the sky were shells as they went over. The rest of the time we were there, you could set your watch by them. Some were around 4 a.m. It didn't make you feel good but it made you go to bed early.

After a night of sleeping with one eye open, both ears tuned in to all the sounds, we got up to a breakfast of cold coffee and hamburger patties. We were told that we would get a hot supper. We did — a canteen of water heated on the manifold of the truck and a hot can of beanie weenies. Then to bed, to be woken up by the whishing noise coming in loud and clear.

The second day for me consisted of setting up the communication center. It was a mobile unit that had to have lines connected. I found out that I was to go out into the field to where the cable was laid and make sure the connections were right. We went to what was called the front line and started the lines back to where we were camped with the headquarters unit. It took us two days of instant coffee and hamburger patties to get the lines in.

On the third day, after a very disturbing night, I began to set up the command post. I was brought a cup of coffee and two pieces of dry bread with salami. I think the beanie weenies tasted better, even when cold. All set up and tested, I turned the post over to the operators and went in search of food. The mess sergeant, a good friend of mine, came out with a plate of all kind of hot goodies. I have often wondered what was on that plate for I have no idea. It had a taste to it and it was hot.

On the fourth day, the people who directed the maneuvers moved in. That morning had started with a misting rain that later turned to snow. Sitting on a mountaintop in the snow, with the swishing of antiaircraft shells over your head at night, is no fun. My nose began to run and my eyes watered. It was the first time in my life that I knew what sinus was. I was sent along with several more to the dispensary at a fort on a mountain outside of Wildflicken. There we were looked at by a doctor who gave us a bottle of A.P.C. pills — all-purpose pills, something like aspirin. Needless to say, the nose kept running and the eyes kept watering.

We arrived back at the command post to find that communication with the front line had gone out. That meant we had to troubleshoot the line all the way back to the front. We started that evening around six o'clock with the understanding that the line would be back up and operating before the next morning.

It was no easy task, with the weather down to zero and the ice pellets hitting you on the face. We found the piece of cable and replaced it. We wound up the piece that was defective and I marked it. I wanted to go over it and find out what had happened, once back at camp. We arrived back at the command post to see a smile on our company commander's face. "Good job," he said. With some hot food we went to bed while the rest of them went to work.

With runny nose and watering eyes, I somehow made it. We were up there at the Russian border for about two weeks. I began to wonder if I would ever see any sunshine again. We took up all our cable and moved back from the mountains at Wildflicken to the Rhine River Valley at Worms.

Back at camp, I went to the warehouse and set the cable up and began an inspection. I was about halfway through the roll when I found it. There, shining, was a new tenpenny nail. It had been driven all the way through the roll of cable. I cut the cable to where it could be repaired. Then I took the piece that had the nail in it to the lieutenant in charge of the cable.

He was the oldest officer in our outfit and everyone liked him. I knocked on his door and he said, "Come in." I saluted him and laid the piece of cable in front of him. He slowly picked it up and looked at it. If I live to be 100 I will never forget the look on his face as he pulled the nail out of the cable. Then he said, "By damn to hell, who would do something like that?" I hid a smile and answered, "I have no idea, sir, but I would like to catch him doing it."

It was many more nails in the cable and a lot of frustration before we found out who was driving the nails in the cable. He was a high-ranking officer in charge of overseeing the maneuvers. He would drive the nail in the cable to see if you could find it. I couldn't understand it at the time, but I know it kept us on our toes when we were out in the field.

Lonie Adcock of Rome is a retired Rome Police Department lieutenant. His latest book is "More Memories of the Old Geezer."

City of Rome's first K-9 served half a century ago; Bruno's marker at resting place at City Hall

Posted: Monday, May 11, 2015 1:00 pm

Police dogs Diesel and Axle are forces to be reckoned with on the streets of Rome, unlike the city's first K-9 officer, Bruno.

Diesel, who works with officer Richard Penson, and Axle, paired with officer Joel Stroupe, are expensive, highly trained dogs.

Bruno was a slightly overweight mutt that just started showing up at City Hall back in the 1950s.

Retired Rome police lieutenant Lonie Adcock said no one ever really knew where Bruno stayed during the day — but when it came time for the night shift to report, Bruno was right there.

Those were the days when the police department was in the basement of City Hall.

Bruno

The bronze marker above Bruno's grave along the driveway to the Rome Water Billing office at City Hall tells the story of Rome's first police dog. (Doug Walker, RN-T)

Officer Tommy Simms, who was often assigned to walk the Broad Street beat, adopted Bruno. Every night, Bruno would be at his side. If Simms was not on duty, Adcock said, Bruno would go with whoever was walking the downtown beat.

Adcock recalled one incident where Simms was attending to a drunk and Bruno was flopped down on the sidewalk. A passerby made an off-hand remark about kicking the dog to get it to move out of the way.

"You'd be better off kicking that cop," Adcock said the old drunk shouted.

When Bruno finally died in 1961, a special casket was commissioned for the dog and he was laid to rest on the side of City Hall.

The city manager at the time, Bruce Hamler, took a personal interest in Bruno's funeral service and a **grave marker** is set at the resting place of Rome's first police dog.

GUEST COLUMN: Dreaming of Old River Rhine

Posted: Wednesday, May 27, 2015 6:15 am

I was sitting and thinking … I do a lot of that here lately. I remember good things and some bad. This memory is about an old man I met while stationed in Germany during my stay in the Army.

On Sunday mornings when I had no duty I would go and sit in the park at the Rhine River. There would be a lot of people with kids there, milling around. I would get a bench close to the river, sit and watch the traffic up and down the river. I would watch this old gentleman fish. He would invite me to fish with him. He would tell me that he had an extra rod. Of course I couldn't, because we were not permitted to fish in the river, lakes or any stream of any kind.

Lonie Adcock

I had eaten breakfast and come by the chapel for a while. Then I headed for my favorite place. There was a dock down from where I sat and you could see the boats as they picked up people. This morning was no different than other Sundays.

Lonie Adcock of Rome is a retired Rome Police Department lieutenant. His latest book, "More Memories of the Old Geezer," is now available.

I began to get a little hungry and got up to go to where there was a bakery that sold ham sandwiches on a hard roll. I usually picked me up one, and a sweet roll. Why I did what I did I will never know, but this Sunday I asked for two sandwiches and two rolls. Back then I never ate that much.

With them in hand, I went back and sat down on my favorite bench. The benches were set in a curve that had a fountain in front of them. I had put my sandwiches down after taking one out. I had several bottles of soda pop. I opened one and took a sip. I began to eat the sandwich when a feeling came over me of being watched. I looked around but no one was on the benches but me.

The feeling persisted until I changed to another bench. I had sat on this bench many times and had felt nothing. I still had the feeling, so I stood up and looked around. There on the bench where I had sat was an old man. Where he came from and how long he had been there is still a mystery to me. He sat and stared at the river.

I slowly took a bite and watched the old man. He didn't seem to know that I existed. I ate slowly and watched him. His face was masked in pain. I picked up my food and went over to where he sat. I sat down beside him. He slowly turned his head and looked at me. The lines in his face told me that here was a man who had a rough life. I offered him the other ham sandwich and he reached out slowly and took it. I opened a soda pop and he took it.

We sat in silence eating, neither speaking. I finished off the sandwich and, taking one of the rolls, offered him the other one. We sat in silence for at least a half hour before the old man spoke.

First he thanked me for the food, then he began to talk. He spoke in broken English, throwing in a word of German as he went along. He raised an old, withered, hand and pointed toward the river. "There," he said, "is where the river ran red with blood." I sat still, letting him do the talking. He looked at me and said, "Many of yours and mine countrymen died here on the banks of the river." I had heard the story before but I had nothing else to do but sit and listen.

It went like this: The American forces had the German army on the run. The Germans blew up bridges and every means of crossing the river. Amazingly, the next morning tanks and troops were rolling across the river on pontoon bridges. It was my understanding that a battle was fought there that no one in the city of Worms would ever forget. So many died in the battle that the river ran red with blood.

The old man stopped talking and took a sip from the soda pop. I watched his face; it was laced with pain. He must have had a loved one killed in the battle.

Seeing that he had grown quiet, I turned my attention to a boat load of people who were getting off at the dock. It must have been some kind of church group for they got off and lined up. They filed by where I sat, two by two. When they got by, I turned to where the old man sat. He was gone. There was not a sign of any kind to indicate that he was ever there. I reached over to get the sack the sandwiches came in. You did not throw anything on the ground in the park. I felt the sack and the sandwich was still inside it. I opened the sack and took out the sandwich. It was still wrapped up. The roll and the soda pop were still there. The soda pop had not been opened.

I stood up and looked around. The park was empty, except for the old fisherman who happened to be there. I sat a lot and talked to the old fisherman. I had become friends with him. I picked up the sandwich and the roll and walked over to him. He greeted me with a smile. I handed him the sandwich and the roll along with the soda pop. He took them with a smile. I sat down and began to talk to him.

According to him, when he came up I was sitting straight up on the bench, asleep. I asked him if there was an old man on the bench with me. He answered that I was the only one on the bench. He said, "In fact, you were the only one in the park when I came up."

I stayed for a while and talked to my fisherman buddy. Then I left and went back to the barracks. I made supper and went to the PX with the others. We sat and listened to the juke box. I drank cokes while a lot of the others had a cold one.

I went back to the park a lot of times but never saw the old man again. I would talk to my fisherman buddy while keeping my eyes open. I never saw him again.

What happened must have been a dream. My old fisherman buddy said that I was asleep when he came up. Did I go to sleep and dream about the old man? Why did the old fisherman get a funny look on his face when I questioned him about the old man? Why had I bought double sandwiches and things when I had never done so before, and never did again?

Did you ever have something happen that you could not explain? You search for an answer but never get it. All I will say is if I was asleep and dreaming, the people who got off of that boat and came by me sure did have some pretty frauleins in the crowd. As I remember in my dream the people on the boat were young and wearing swimsuits. And I can still remember the old man telling about the Rhine River running red with blood.

If it was a dream, it has stayed with me for quite a few years. The face of the old man is still in my mind with the look of anguish all over it.

Lonie Adcock of Rome is a retired Rome Police Department lieutenant. His latest book is "More Memories of the Old Geezer."

Sponsored From Around the Web

GUEST COLUMN: Scarecrow Joe and Raggedy Ann

Posted: Wednesday, June 10, 2015 6:15 am

I like to go back though the years and think about people I have met that left their memories with me. I will start out with a fellow that everyone up and down Broad Street called Scarecrow Joe. I met him when I walked a beat on Broad Street. He would come down early in the morning and have his beer for breakfast. I never could understand how anyone could drink beer for breakfast.

The first time I recall seeing him I was working traffic at Second and Broad. The 5 o'clock traffic was mean. It would back up across the South Rome Bridge. Second Avenue from Sears to Broad would be two solid lanes of traffic, bumper to bumper.

After fighting the traffic for about two hours all you felt like doing was going somewhere and sitting down. It didn't work that way, for the Cotton Block gang started to gather about the time you left the street.

Lonie Adcock

Lonie Adcock of Rome is a retired Rome Police Department lieutenant. His latest book, "More Memories of the Old Geezer," is now available.

I had gone up to the Victory Cafe for something to eat and felt better when I headed for the Cotton Block. At that time there were five places in the Cotton Block that sold beer. Most of them were full from around 8 o'clock until midnight. As I crossed the street I noticed this tall skinny fellow going into the Bumble Bee Cafe. I hadn't ever seen him before so I decided to give him the once-over.

I walked into the Cafe and stepped just inside the door. I looked the crowd over and noticed that the tall skinny fellow was sitting on a stool drinking a beer. The owner came up to me and started to talk. I motioned to him and asked who he was. She couldn't tell me his name, only that everyone in the Cotton Block called him Scarecrow Joe.

He needed a haircut and a shave. His clothes were raggedy and the top of one shoe was cut out. I looked him over from head to toe. I noticed that his foot that had the cutaway shoe looked smaller. I moved into a position to look him over. He had an artificial leg.

The owner of the cafe told me he had lost a leg in Korea. Since he had come back home, he stayed high on alcohol. He drank his beer, paid and started toward me. He then stopped and looked me over from head to toe. He moved toward the door and, as he passed, said, "Looking good, Adcock." I turned but he had got out the door and was headed up the street.

Time passed and I never got the chance to ask him how he knew me. With his face covered in a beard, his raggedy clothes and a smell like a pig pen, I never talked to him. I went in to work one day to find Scarecrow sitting out back with several others who were working out a fine. As I approached him, he got up and walked away. I knew that he didn't want to talk to me. I never pushed the issue.

I would see him, and at times would have to lock him up for being drunk. Once I looked at the book and saw his name — and then I knew why he didn't want to talk to me.

It was one of those hot Sunday mornings when everything was quiet. My partner, who I will call Pete, had a warrant to search a house on Smith Street for white whiskey. We pulled into the yard and got out. One of the dirtiest women that I had ever seen sat on the front porch. She started to get up but Pete stopped her. As I got close to her I felt my stomach turn over. I moved over out of her way.

Pete showed her the warrant and told her what we were looking for. She said a word that I will not repeat and sat back down. I walked into the house. It was filthy.

The floor was full of all kind of junk and paper wrappings. She would eat and throw the wrappings on the floor. In the kitchen, roach bugs were all over the floor. The sink was full of maggots on what looked like raw chicken. I headed for the back door and jumped from the porch to the yard, gagging. I had never seen anything like it before. I let it come up and walked over and sat down on a pile of wood.

I was letting my stomach settle when I noticed something shiny in among the wood. I reached down and pulled out a gallon can. I opened it and took a smell. It almost took off the top of my head. Some of what we called rotgut was in the can. I put the top back on, walked over to the porch and called Pete. He came out on the porch and I handed it to him. He took the top off and gave it a big smell. A funny look came on his face and he shook his head and said, "Rotgut."

We took her to the old jail that was on the river at that time. I called her Raggedy Ann, but when we walked her into the jail one of the deputies said, "Watch out, here comes The Maggot." We booked her in and the jailer told a woman matron, "Take her up and see that she gets a shower." Pete and I went back to the station to clean out the car. As we pulled out from the jail I noticed that they were taking the Scarecrow out of a car and into jail.

A few years passed and I went into plainclothes as an investigator. I had just come in when the head of the investigators gave me an address and sent me to talk to the people who lived there about a burglar. On East Sixth Avenue, where there is now businesses, there was a row of houses. I checked the address and pulled into the yard. A man was sitting on the porch. I asked him was he the one who called. He said he was and began to tell me about having some stuff stolen from a shed in back of his house.

I then asked him his name. He laughed and said, "I was waiting for this." He gave me the name of someone I had gone to school with." I looked at him and he said, "But you know me better as Scarecrow." That floored me. He was dressed neat, with a clean shave and a haircut. He didn't looked anything like the Scarecrow.

He got up and walked over to the door, limping. He opened the screen and called, "Ann, come out here. I want you to meet someone from way back." He sat back down and I watched as the door opened. A woman came out on the porch and looked at me and said, "Officer Adcock, I believe."

I didn't recognize her at first, for here stood a beautiful woman in her 30s. She could have put a lot of younger ones to shame with her looks and figure. She laughed out loud and said, "You don't remember me?" I shook my head. I couldn't place her. "The deputies at the jail used to call me Maggot," she said. My mouth must had been hanging open for she laughed again and said, "Close your mouth before a bug gets in it." I sat and talked to them for a while.

I marvel at how they had turned their lives around. Scarecrow had a job driving a delivery truck in the city. Raggedy Ann had a job at a department store. They had met at the county jail and fell in love. When they got out of jail they got married. I kept up with them until I retired from the police department. The last time I saw and talked to them was at a hamburger place.

Scarecrow and Ann, if you are still living and read this, I want you to know that I admire you for the way you turned out.

Lonie Adcock of Rome is a retired Rome Police Department lieutenant. His latest book is "More Memories of the Old Geezer."

Sponsored From Around the Web

GUEST COLUMN: Going on and on about irritating things

Posted: Wednesday, June 24, 2015 6:15 am

There are a lot of things that irritate me.

You get your food at a restaurant and sit down. You take a bite. And the person sitting across from you pulls a napkin and start to blow his nose. He then uses the napkin to wipe his fingers.

The person then takes out his cellphone and starts to talk loud enough for everyone to hear him. With not quite half of my food eaten, he then begins to cough, open-mouth, into the air.

Looking around for a ball bat or a big long stick but unable to find either, I slowly wrap up my food and get up to throw it into the trash can. As I open the door to leave, he lets out one of those coughs spraying the air with germs. He has a napkin in his hand but doesn't have time to lower his telephone.

You go to a lecture and find a seat to where you can both hear and see the speaker. Just before you get comfortable, in come the dignitaries. All seats have been taken. They then begin to shove everyone back and put chairs in front of you.

Lonie Adcock

Lonie Adcock of Rome is a retired Rome Police Department lieutenant. His latest book, "More Memories of the Old Geezer," is now available.

In come several people weighing somewhere around 300 pounds each. When they sit down, your sight has been blocked — and the smell of alcohol floats back to you. The speaker starts to talk, and so do the ones in front of you; they talk more than the one you came to hear.

When it's all over you look down at your notepad. Nothing on it. Maybe you got it on your recorder … but all you have is the conversation of the latecomers who were placed in front of you.

I remember, way back in school at the old Boys High, a boy named John. He was a Class A student. He always had his homework and was very pleasant to all the teachers. All the teachers thought John was the model student. Always "yes, ma'am" and "no ma'am" and homework in hand.

Now that model student had one habit that did not go over with the other students. John was a bully. He would find a small boy or girl and, for that day, he made life miserable for them. When someone tried to tell the teachers what John was doing they were not believed.

In my growing up, I was what people referred to as tall and lanky. That meant tall with very little meat on me. I knew that in a rough and tumble with someone the size of John I would not have a chance.

I took my old Barlow and began to make me a weapon for the day John decided to jump me. I got a stick and whittled it to fit in to my hand. I made a round end on it. A good poke in the stomach with one of the ends would made you think. A round end to the face and you didn't want any more.

I had a friend who I will call Jack. Jack was small. He was about half as tall as me and weighed less. I lived on what was the short end of Avenue D back then. I would go down West Ninth Street to North Fifth and get with a crowd and walk to school. I watched John and knew that he was going to make Little Jack his next victim.

I got Jack to go home with me that evening and showed him how to use the weapon that I called The Equalizer. I worked all evening showing Little Jack what to do. With my equalizer in his pocket, ready for the next day, Jack went home.

Early the next morning we all met on North Fifth and started to school. John joined us along in the area where the Fifth Avenue Church was located. He ran up behind Jack and shoved Jack to the ground.

I knew it was coming. He always did his foul deed before he got to school. If it didn't happen on the school ground the teachers couldn't do anything about it. But the teachers all knew what was happening when the smaller boys came in with a bloody nose.

Jack got up slowly with his hand in his back pocket. Then John did the wrong thing. He grabbed Jack by the front of the shirt and stuck his face in Jack's face. I saw it when it connected above John's right eye. He dropped to his knees with blood pouring down his face. Little Jack was so scared that he kept swinging at John. John got to his feet and ran down the street in front of the church.

I got Jack settled down and we went on to school. John didn't come to school that day. As I recall, John became a good boy and didn't pick on any more small boys.

Another thing I have never liked is for someone to come up and start messing with my hair. Call it a phobia or whatever — don't mess with my hair. And you can talk to me all day telling me how wrong I am but do not stick your finger in my face. A finger in my face with ugly words gets my blood pressure up.

Also, have you ever been somewhere and heard loud vulgar language? You look around and there, standing where everyone can see them, will be two people talking loud enough for the whole world to hear. Every word is a cuss word or some type of vulgar word. I think that a person who can't talk without using foul language should stay at home, away from people.

Last, but not least, is the person who is telling you something and keeps saying "you know." No, I don't know. If I did, I would not have asked him. That's a lot like the person who is telling you something and keeps saying "blah, blah, blah."

I could probably go on and on about the things that irritate me. I will stop and let you think about things that irritate you.

Why do people blow their nose when someone is trying to eat? Why will someone cough all over you and not cover their mouth? Why do people talk when they go to hear someone speak? And why does someone want to jump on someone else? It's not always the big guy on the small one. In some cases it's a small guy that wants to get a reputation for being bad and whipping up on big guys.

I've often wondered why anyone says "blah, blah" and "you know." Do you know?

Lonie Adcock of Rome is a retired Rome Police Department lieutenant. His latest book is "More Memories of the Old Geezer."

Sponsored From Around the Web

GUEST COLUMN: Born on the Fourth of July

Posted: Thursday, July 2, 2015 6:15 am

This is one of those stories that was told to me down though the years as I was growing up. I have searched all the evidence that was given to me and came to the conclusion that it must be true. I will try to tell it to you and let you decide if it is fact or fiction.

In the Depression years there was no work so most people lived on farms and grew their food. What was left over was traded for other kinds of goods that kept the body going. This took place in Bartow County — Kingston, Georgia.

Where the old schoolhouse now sits there was a house, and between there and the town, on both sides of the road, was the land farmed by my father, Landum B. Adcock. At that time Landum had his wife and three little girls to feed, so it was early to bed and early to rise to keep the family fed.

The three girls were Zonie, Lillie and Gracy. They would tell me this and would not have smiles on their faces, so it must have been true.

Lonie Adcock

Lonie Adcock of Rome is a retired Rome Police Department lieutenant. His latest book, "More Memories of the Old Geezer," is now available.

My father had gone to the field early one morning to see what needed to be done to his crop. I was told what was needed was rain, for this was one of them hot July days. My father was in the field and the girls were in the yard playing when my mother came to the door and hollered for them to come inside.

That scared them, for their mother seemed to be hurting and had laid down on the bed.

"You," she told Zonie, "run down to town and get Doctor Burton and tell him to hurry."

"You," she told Lillie, "go down to the field and get your father. Hurry now."

The girls ran out the door and Gracy, who was just a baby, began to cry for she thought her mother was going to die. Mother soon got her calmed down and she sat by the bed, holding her hand.

Doctor Burton had an old Ford car, so it didn't take him just a few minutes and he was pulling into the yard with Zonie hurrying him into the house. Lillie and my father were close behind.

This is the part I will leave up to you to judge whether it is fact or fiction.

Doctor Burton ran the girls out onto the porch, telling them their mother was going to be all right. They told me they peeped down the hallway but all they could see was a little black bag that the doctor had brought with him. Then he reached and got the bag and put it out of sight. They tried to imagine what he had in that little black bag.

Their father came out and went to the kitchen, got a big pan of water and carried it in to the room. Then, to the surprise of the girls, they heard a baby cry.

They would laugh as they told me the story, saying they thought that was impossible for there were no babies around. Then they heard it again. It was a baby crying. When they were told they could come in and see their little brother, they knew exactly where it had come from. The doctor carried a baby around in his black bag.

The way it was told to me was that, when they went inside, the baby was on the bed with their mother and the black bag sat on the floor empty. Picking up the bag and smiling at them, Doctor Burton left. Without a doubt the baby had been in the bag, but back then everyone knew storks brought babies and dropped them down the chimney to people who wanted them. The fireplace was closed off for the summer, so the stork must have given him to the doctor to bring.

Whether the stork had been lazy and fell down on his job or the doctor just happened to have a spare, I came into this world on July the Fourth, 1930. The evidence is in. You be the judge — fact or fiction?

I was told that my middle name was taken from Doctor Burton. I accepted the fact that I came into the family by way of the doctor's little black bag. Many years later I went on the Rome Police Department. I was promoted to the investigator department after a brief period of time.

A patrol officer called me one day to come and look at what they had found during a car stop. I went to headquarters and checked with the officers. The car was full of stolen goods. I began a check for the owners and gave back most of the stuff, but I remember that a little bag and an old-fashioned walking stick was left.

I checked the bag out and, to my surprise, found a metal tag with the name Doctor R.E. Burton in the bag. I looked the walking stick over but found no name or anything to identify it.

I placed the little black bag and the walking stick in my car when I got off that night. The next day I went to Kingston, to see if the doctor was still there. I found his office and talked to the lady who was out front. She showed me back to where he was. I had been told all my life that the good doctor had lost a leg. He sat at a desk — he was getting up in years.

The lady told him my name and he studied me for a few moments. He smiled when I told him why I was there. I put the bag on his desk and he smiled again. He said "someone broke into my office and took my bag. They used it to put inside what they stole from my office."

"Had that old bag a long time," he said, placing it on the floor behind him.

Then he turned to me and asked my father's name. I told him and he smiled, and said Landum was a good man. "It's been a while, but I remember Landum's first boy," he said. "He lived where the schoolhouse is now."

I told him I was that boy and we talked for a while. I left feeling that I had indeed been blessed to have met the doctor who brought me into this world. The one thing that I have always regretted was not asking him if there were any babies in that bag that I had brought to him.

Lonie Adcock of Rome is a retired Rome Police Department lieutenant. His latest book is "More Memories of the Old Geezer."

Sponsored From Around the Web

GUEST COLUMN: The old oak tree

Posted: Wednesday, July 8, 2015 6:00 am

I have written a lot of stories about strange happenings. When they are read, the people will come up to me and ask, "Do you believe in ghosts?" I answer, "There are strange things that have happened in my life."

I am looked at by some people in a strange way. There are more people who believe in ghosts but will not admit it. Some ask, "Have you ever seen a ghost?" I answer, "Have you?" Some will say yes and some will say no. I try to let you draw your own conclusions as to what I write. Unless I specify that what I am writing is fiction, it is based on facts.

Take, for instance, what happened on a Saturday night hay ride.

The driver of the wagon took us up to a big oak tree on Park Road and told us a ghost story. We talked about it and decided to bring our group of people back as soon as possible. All the next week

Lonie Adcock

Lonie Adcock of Rome is a retired Rome Police Department lieutenant. His latest book, "More Memories of the Old Geezer," is now available.

the excitement grew at the thought of getting a good scare out of the girls. Duke and I had been planning to go to the Grand Ole Opry in Nashville on the next Saturday night, so we told them to be in the park after we got off from work on Friday and we would visit the old oak tree.

We talked about it all week, and when Friday rolled around Carlton and the girls were waiting for us. It was just getting dark when Duke and I got to the park. I moved from the front seat into the back. They began to load up. We had a car full of people. We headed for Park Road.

As usual, everyone was talking at once. It sounded like a free-for-all party. I knew that once we got to the big oak tree everyone would be as quiet as a mouse. And when Duke turned from the road and started up the dirt road to the tree, you could have heard a pin drop inside the car. Duke circled around and turned the car facing the road.

With the motor off, I opened the door next to me and said, "OK, everybody out." Very quietly every one began to get out. I walked over to the big oak where I had stood the night of the hay ride. I felt the presence of someone close to me. I knew who it was, for she was always next to me at all of our ghost trips.

I looked at her and she said, "Do you remember what we saw from the road when we were on the hay ride?" I remember nodding and saying, "Your imagination was working overtime." What she said then has stayed with me down though the years — "You can deny things you see and feel to others, but inside you know."

I remember taking her hand and walking over to the tree and putting it against it. I don't think either one of us was prepared for what happened next. I looked at her and she looked at me. Her eyes in the moonlight looked like two big marbles. I dropped her hand out of mine and stepped back. We had heard a voice and it didn't sound like anyone in our crowd.

We walked over to where the others were. I had cold chills running up and down my back. The hair on my arms was standing straight up. As we moved away from the tree I heard the voice again. I turned back to tree and stopped. We both stood still, listening. We turned back facing the others to see what they were doing.

I sat down on the fender of the car and listened to a story that Carlton was telling. We all knew that his story was fiction. Carlton could spin a good ghost story and when we went on a ghost hunt he had one ready.

Francis and I looked at each other and smiled. We remember some funny situation involving him. We were at a cemetery once and we found him lying beside a tombstone, moaning. He claimed that a ghost had thrown him over the tombstone to the ground. Everyone had got a big laugh out of that one. Did it really happen the way he told it? He would raise his right hand and swear to it.

I leaned over and whispered in Francis' ear. I told her to get the girls over to the tree. I would tell them what the driver of the hay ride wagon had told us. Francis moved in and began to talk to them. They followed her and we all moved over to the big oak tree. Once under it, the old chills and standing-up hair took over again.

"Listen up," I told them. I then began to tell about the woman who lived in the area. She had come up missing. A search party found her — she had been tied to the tree and killed. Her body was found several days after she had been killed. We had been told by the wagon driver that an escaped convict had done it, he was caught and punished.

If there was any truth to this story, I never knew. I will say that there was something going on under the tree.

I moved back over to the car and sat down on the fender. The crowd was milling around. I watched Carlton as he laid it on real thick to the girls. Francis had come over and we were discussing what we had heard when one of the girls let out a scream. I jumped down from the fender and ran to where she was.

I got to her and she was pointing to the ground beside the tree. I took out a penlight from my shirt pocket and shined it on the ground. There lay Duke, as still as if he was dead. I knelt down beside him and saw he was still breathing. He seemed to be all right, then I shined the light on his face.

He had blood on his forehead from a cut. I told Francis to go to the car and get some napkins from the dash. With Carlton's help I wwgot him sitting up. I wiped his forehead with the napkins. I asked Carlton could he drive and he said no. I could drive but had no license. A cup of leftover ice was handed to me and I began to wipe Duke's face with it. The cold mixture of Coke and water did the job, for he opened his eyes and began to moan. We got him up and back to the car.

While the others took care of him I walked back over to the tree. I felt a presence and turned. Francis was, as I used to say, in my back pocket. I remember her saying, "You didn't think I was going to let you come back over here by yourself." We stood and listened to the sound of the night.

Somewhere off in the distance a hoot owl was sounding off. Then, from the tree, a sound came. It sounded like the voice of someone in pain. Francis grabbed my arm and began to pull me back to where the crowd was.

Duke was able to drive so we all loaded up and headed back to the park to let the girls out. Once the girls were out Duke drove me home. We parked in front of the house and I said, "OK, tell me what happened." He sat still for a few seconds and then turned to where I could see his face.

"I will tell you because you will believe me," he said. "I walked behind the tree and the next thing I knew, you were washing my face with wet napkins. I have no idea what hit me."

We let it go at that, for if he had known what hit him he would have told me. The next day he had a knot with a cut in the middle of it. I remember that the last time I saw him he had a scar on his forehead.

Lonie Adcock of Rome is a retired Rome Police Department lieutenant. His latest book is "More Memories of the Old Geezer."

Sponsored From Around the Web

GUEST COLUMN: My first French lesson

Posted: Wednesday, July 22, 2015 6:15 am

While sitting and listening to good Georgia Mountain Music, a memory came back to me that brought a smile to my face. It was a memory of a 12-year-old boy and his first appearance on a stage in front of a group of people. As I remember the incident, it still brings a chill down my back.

Back then I could hold my own with the people I knew, but to stand up in front of a group of people you don't know, it was frightening. In later years I grew out of being bothered by people that I didn't know. Try being a policeman and it will bring a lot of things out of you.

I was in the sixth grade, going to Neely School. It was close to the end of the first year that I had gone to Neely. I had got to know all my classmates and was at ease with them. I remember that we had Mrs. Smith for a teacher.

Lonie Adcock

Lonie Adcock of Rome is a retired Rome Police Department lieutenant. His latest book, "More Memories of the Old Geezer," is now available.

You know how things sort of slow down close to the end of the year. Homework had got to be none and the teachers were just waiting for the year to end. I thought that we had it made, but the teachers got together and decided to put on a play.

We had been over to the Rome High Hilltoppers before. They had a big auditorium with loudspeakers and a stage. We listened as Mrs. Smith gave out the names of those who would be in the play. Since there was only one person whose name started with an A, I was the first one she called.

We were told, as our name was called, to come to the front and pick up a paper with our part on it. I walked real slow, hoping that she would change her mind and forget me. She handed me a sheet of paper and I hurried back to my desk. I looked at the paper and there was a song written on it. I was stunned. Me sing? I could not ever remember singing.

With the parts given out she began to tell us a story about an American girl who visited France and how she won the hearts of the French people. I was to play the part of a shy boy who would get off in the woods and sing. The girl would ask that I sing for her after hearing me. I had to sing to her, but a boy everyone called Stinky would win her heart. Quite a letdown for me, but I was determine to learn the song and sing. The weekend was coming up and we were told to learn our parts, and on Monday we would go in to rehearsal.

My mother could not understand what had come over me. I walked around over the weekend singing. She had never heard me sing before. Think about a 12-year-old boy whose voice was beginning to change, who never sang, walking around for two days singing. I stayed out in the swing under the big tree in the yard most of the weekend.

Monday morning and I was eager to show Mrs. Smith and all my classmates what I could do. I got with my usual people and we headed for school. Once inside, everybody was excited. That is, everybody but me. I had my part down pat. We went into rehearsal and it went well. Then my turn came.

With all the confidence in the world I went into my song. I finished and waited for Mrs. Smith to ring a small bell telling me to move out and let the next one start. I looked at her; she looked at me. I waited and finally she said, "Young man, are you going to stop in the middle of your song or will you finish it?" My mouth must have fallen open for she said, "You only sang half of your song."

I mumbled something to the effect that I sang what was on the paper. "Go get the paper and bring it to me," she said. I got the paper and handed it to her. She turned the paper over and said, "here." I took the paper and looked at it. It had never occurred to me that the gibbish on the back side of the paper was part of the song. I looked at it. I have always been a fairly decent reader, but I could not read and understand what was on the back of the paper.

I walked back to my desk and sat down. They were still in rehearsal but my mind was on the gibbish on the paper. At the end of the day she told me that I would stay after school and she would teach me the rest of my song.

I sat still as everyone left the classroom. I had looked at the paper, not understanding a word of it. The classroom empty, Mrs. Smith sat down at her desk and told me to come and sit in a chair she had placed in front of her. I sat down and she reached for the paper. Then I got my first and only lesson in French.

I tried as hard as I could to say the words in French the same way as she did. To this day, I will always believe that I spoke French different to her. She kept me for almost an hour, letting me go with these words. "You learn that song by tomorrow for we meet at the Boys High School in the morning and the play will start."

I know that on my way home the people that saw me must have thought I was a nut loose from the funny farm. Picture a barefooted boy in overalls singing what he thought was French while going down the street.

The next morning I put on my Sunday-go-to-church outfit, wearing shoes, and headed for the Boys High School. I grabbed a biscuit and filled it with sorghum syrup. With syrup all over my hands, I used my handkerchief to wipe them clean. I put the sticky handkerchief in my back pocket.

When I got to school I was rushed backstage with the others. We were sat in a row of chairs in the order that we were to appear on stage. I was the last one to appear on stage. It ended with me.

I really enjoyed it. I played the part of a bashful French boy who would go out in the woods and sing to the birds and animals. The American girl was given a going-home party and had asked for the boy who sang in the wood to sing his song for her. I was told that I strutted a little when I walked out on stage. On cue, I started to sing my song:

"Are you sleeping, are you sleeping, Brother Jack, Brother Jack. Morning bells are ringing, morning bells are ringing. Ding Dang Dong, Ding Dang Dong."

Now my French version:

"Fer a Jacko, Fer a Jacko, dough mae boo, dough mae boo. Sana la tena, sana la tena. Ding Dang Dong, Ding Dang Dong."

The audience gave me a big hand and, like I was told to do, I bowed and thanked them. Then as I hurried back to my seat the audience got louder — and they were laughing, and the kids in the crowd were hollowing and, as told, I went back out on stage with a big smile on my face and bowed. I again thanked them. I sat down and the crowd got quiet and the play was over.

We were let out for the day and I started home with the rest. All my friends were telling me how good I was and that gave me the big head. Then one of them started to laugh. I told him to let me in on the joke. Then I was told that when I had bowed to the audience, instead of saying "thank you," I had said "Amen." Then I was told that when I went back the second time I had bowed and, loud and clear, I said "Amen" into the mike.

I remember that, later, my mother wanted to know what I had put in my pocket that stuck my handkerchief to it. She said she had to put the pants into boiling water to get the handkerchief free.

Lonie Adcock of Rome is a retired Rome Police Department lieutenant. His latest book is "More Memories of the Old Geezer."

Sponsored From Around the Web

GUEST COLUMN: Georgia's bad boy: Doc Holliday

Posted: Wednesday, August 5, 2015 6:30 am

I guess every state in the United States has had a bad boy. Georgia's was Doc Holliday.

Henry B. Holliday was a trained pharmacist who served in several wars. After serving in the Mexican War he returned to his home to Griffin, Georgia, with an orphaned Mexican boy. On Jan. 8, 1849, he married Alice Jane McKay and within a year had a daughter, who died in infancy. On Aug. 14,1851, John Henry (Doc) Holliday was born.

In 1857 Major Holliday moved to Lowndes County and quickly became Valdosta's leading citizen. He served two terms as mayor. He also served in other functions and offices of government in Valdosta and Lowndes County.

When Doc was just 15, his mother died of consumption. Consumption was later known as tuberculosis. Doc and his mother had a close relationship. Her death was a hard blow. His father remarried a short time later.

Lonie Adcock

Lonie Adcock of Rome is a retired Rome Police Department lieutenant. His latest book, "More Memories of the Old Geezer," is now available.

The family's status in the community — and the fact that a cousin had started the Pennsylvania College of Dentistry — probably encouraged Doc to enroll in dental school. On March 1, 1872, he was conferred a degree as doctor of dental surgery. He began his work as a dentist in Atlanta.

Though an educated and respected man, Doc was a hot-tempered Southerner. It is said that when some people were swimming in his favorite hole he grabbed his gun and began to fire over their heads. Shots were fired back, but no one was hit. This seems to be the first account of Doc's love for the gun.

Shortly after starting his dental practice he discovered he had tuberculosis. His adopted Mexican brother also was diagnosed with the disease and later died from it. Doc was told he had a short time to live and encouraged to move to a dry climate. In October 1883, he packed his bags and headed for Dallas, Texas.

He worked with another dentist in Dallas. As the coughing spells increased, he was forced to find another way to make a living. Doc was an unusual character, being an educated and refined man. He was fluent in Latin, played the piano and was a natty dresser. He displayed the manners of a Southern gentleman.

His intelligence made him a natural at gambling and it became his means of support. He was an active poker and faro dealer, moody, and a heavy drinker. With the knowledge of his impending death, he had no fear of death. He knew the occupation of a gambler was risky. He began to practice with his gun.

The first account of a gunfight occurred on Jan. 2, 1875. No one was hurt. Most of the people thought it was amusing, until a few days later when Doc got into another. This time, Doc killed a prominent citizen.

Fleeing Dallas with a posse behind him, he ended up in Jacksboro, Texas. Doc found a job dealing faro, with a gun in a shoulder holster and one on his hip. Jacksboro was a wild and lawless town. Doc also carried a knife. He was involved in three more gunfights in a short time. He left one man dead, but no action was taken against him.

In the summer of 1876, a disagreement led to violence. He killed a soldier from Fort Richardson. This brought in the U.S. government. A reward was offered for his capture and he was pursued by the Army, Texas Rangers and the U.S. Marshals. There also were bounty hunters looking for him.

Doc fled for his life to the Kansas territory, now Colorado. On his way he left three more bodies in the wake. He settled down in Denver, taking the name of Tom Mackey. While dealing faro he got into an argument with another gambler. Doc nearly cut his head off with his lethal knife. The gambler survived, his face and neck terribly mutilated. This forced Doc to run again — first to Wyoming and then to New Mexico. He finally went back to Texas, where he met Wyatt Earp and Big Nose Kate.

Big Nose Kate did have a prominent nose; her other features were quite lovely. She was a prostitute by trade. When asked if she liked her trade, she would say that she liked her business. Kate and Doc became friends. When he was seen in Dodge City, Kate was often with him.

In Dodge City, Doc saved Wyatt Earp's life when a gunman drew behind Earp's back. Doc yelled a warning, drew and shot the man. Wyatt Earp had several brothers. They were a close family. Many experts believe that the Earp brothers became replacements for the family Doc had left in Georgia. Wyatt, Morgan and Virgil Earp were friends with Doc for the rest of their lives.

Doc Holliday became well-known in the West. He became even more famous after taking part in the gunfight at the O.K. Corral with Wyatt, Morgan and Virgil Earp. As they came to the corral, Wyatt demanded that the Clantons surrender. Shots were fired and, when it was over, Billy

Clanton, Frank McLaury and Tom McLaury were dead. Ike Clanton had run away. Morgan and Virgil Earp were wounded. Neither Doc nor Wyatt were hurt.

Enemies of the Earp brothers wanted a trial. The Earp brothers and Doc Holliday were arrested. The jury found them innocent. A few months later, a gunman killed Morgan Earp. Doc and Wyatt began to hunt the killer. They killed several men who were known to be involved.

It is not known how many killings Doc was involved in. Some say as many as 30, some say closer to eight. History will tell you that Doc was arrested several times, mostly for playing illegal games of chance. The few times he faced a criminal charge he was found not guilty. Often the charges were dismissed because he was defending himself.

Doc Holliday may have won at cards and gunfights but he could not win against tuberculosis. On Nov. 8, 1887, he died in his bed in the little city of Glenwood, Colorado. He was 36 years old.

Wyatt Earp said of Doc Holliday, "I found him a loyal friend and good company. He was a dentist whom necessity had made a gambler; a gentleman whom disease had made a vagabond; a philosopher whom life had made a caustic wit; a long, lean blonde fellow nearly dead with consumption and at the same time the most skillful gambler and nerviest, speediest, deadliest man with a six-gun I ever knew."

Lonie Adcock of Rome is a retired Rome Police Department lieutenant. His latest book is "More Memories of the Old Geezer."

Sponsored From Around the Web

GUEST COLUMN: The ghost in the cemetery

Posted: Wednesday, August 19, 2015 6:15 am

This happened while I was working the detective division on a Sunday evening when everything had quieted down. I had just come in when the telephone rang.

The dispatcher said someone on the line wanted to talk to me. I asked if they had called my name. "No, they wanted to talk to a detective." I asked, "Is this one of your funny calls?" "No," the dispatcher answered.

I picked up the telephone and said, "Detective Adcock, may I help you?" A slight hesitation and, again, I said, "Detective Adcock may I help you?"

A cold chill went up my back when a voice whispered, "Do you investigate murders?" Then, before I could say anything, he whispered, "This happened a long time ago."

"How long ago," I asked.

"This happened to a soldier during World War II," he whispered.

Lonie Adcock

Lonie Adcock of Rome is a retired Rome Police Department lieutenant. His latest book, "More Memories of the Old Geezer," is now available.

If this happened during WWII, that was just too far back. I knew that to find records would be just about impossible. But he had my curiosity up enough that I wanted to know more.

"Tell me what happened," I said.

Still whispering, he told me.

This was supposed to have taken place in a cemetery at a church on Callier Springs Road. He said that during the war he had a friend that was in the Army with him. They came home on leave before shipping out. They met a girl that his friend fell in love with. She was a married woman.

She lived on Callier Springs Road and they would meet at the rear of the cemetery. There were no houses at the back of the cemetery, just a wooded area. A few days before they had to go back to camp his friend went to meet this girl. He never saw his friend again.

When he got out of the Army and came back home, he tried to find out about his friend. He talked to his friend's parents, who said the Army said he went AWOL.

"That was when we were home before shipping out," he said. "I know that he never went AWOL. He was murdered by this girl's husband."

I interrupted him. "How do you know that he was murdered?"

He said he talked to the woman's mother after he got back. "She said that the woman and my friend met at the back of the cemetery and her husband caught them and killed him," he went on. "He took her and moved up north somewhere. Her mother said that she was up north for only a few months until she got word that her daughter was dead."

He paused and I waited for him to start talking again. He took a deep breath and said, "My friend's body was buried up there somewhere behind the cemetery. I looked but could never find the place. I know he was murdered because he was never heard of again. He just disappeared from the face of this earth."

I stopped him by asking, "Did they ever find out what the girl died of?"

"No. She was buried up north and he was never heard of again. He never came back to Rome, but she does."

That threw me. "She comes back to Rome? I thought you said that she was buried up north."

A pause, then, "Mister, she comes back to the cemetery at certain nights and walks around looking for her lover."

"You are telling me that on certain nights she can be seen in the cemetery?"

"Yes."

"What nights would that be?" I asked. "Am I to understand from you that she comes back from the dead?"

"Yes. On a moonlit night she can be seen at the edge of the cemetery looking for her lover. Most of the time she is seen will be on a Saturday or Sunday night, when the moon is shining bright."

I remember that the line went dead and I sat for a minute holding the telephone to my ear. Then I put the telephone on the hook and got up. I went up to the dispatcher and stood looking at him.

He began to laugh and I shook my head saying, "Where did you find that one?"

"He calls up here every time we have a full moon. He tells me the same story over and over. I thought I would let you hear it and see what you thought of it," the dispatcher said.

I shook my head. I must admit he had my attention, but when he started to tell me that she comes back and walks the cemetery, that got me. "Do you believe in ghosts," I asked.

"I don't know," he answered. "I have seen and heard things I didn't know what they were."

I asked him, "Why don't I call the captain in and see if he will let you go with me to the cemetery?" He got a funny look on his face and the other dispatcher started to laugh. "Why, Pete," she said. "I do believe that you are afraid." Pete smiled and said, "Call the captain and I will get ready to go."

The captain came in and I explained to him what I wanted. "Come on," he said. "I will go with you and Pete."

We got in the captain's car, with Pete driving and the captain in the back seat. In those days patrol cars did not have cages in them. On the way over to the cemetery I found out that the captain believed in ghosts, and he would hunt out places that were supposed to be haunted. I felt better knowing there were two others with me.

We pulled the patrol car in back of the church, where we had a good view of the rear of the cemetery. With the lights out, we watched the cemetery and the woods where the girl was supposed to appear. We sat quiet, no one speaking. Then I saw something just at the edge of the woods. Pete sat still, but I knew he had seen what I had.

Then the captain spoke. "Pete, did you see those lights moving around out there?" Pete didn't move or say a word. The captain asked me and I answered, "I saw them, Captain. They are called cemetery lights."

I remember I got out of the car and walked over to the end of the church where I could see the cemetery. The captain came up beside me and stood watching. He touched my shoulder and pointed toward the woods where the murder was supposed to have happened.

Was it a cemetery light that we saw or was it the girl hunting her lover? I will call it a cemetery light, even though it was of a different color than the others. We stayed there several hours, watching the lights, and punching each other whenever a different color appeared among them.

On the way back the captain and I talked about the lights. Pete sat still and listened.

I had several more conversations with the man on the telephone. I checked a few newspapers back around that time but never found any information. Was the different-color light the girl hunting her lover or just cemetery lights? I will never know, for I never went back to the cemetery to find out.

Lonie Adcock of Rome is a retired Rome Police Department lieutenant. His latest book is "More Memories of the Old Geezer."

GUEST COLUMN: Stories old folks told

Posted: Wednesday, September 2, 2015 6:15 am

Back in the days that I grew up in, it was quite different from today. Very few houses had electricity. Kerosene lamps furnished most of your light at night. Most of the radios were powered by batteries. They didn't pick up many stations because there was so much interference at night.

On Saturdays, the young ones would gather around with the older people and listen to stories told by the mothers.

There was all kind of stories told. My favorite was the ghost stories. The story that I am going to write about was told to us by the old folks at that time. Were these stories true? Can't say. Most of the time the one telling the story would say they knew the people that it happened to. We took it for granted that it was the truth. I have no way of knowing if it really happened or not.

Lonie Adcock

Lonie Adcock of Rome is a retired Rome Police Department lieutenant. His latest book, "More Memories of the Old Geezer," is now available.

The story goes this way: There were some iron ore mines operating in or around Canton. As far as I can remember, they were called the Little Dinky Mines. It could have been just Dinky Mines. It seemed that the people in the area depended on the mines for a living. Then the bad news came: The mines were closing down. The people began to look around for some place to move.

According to my mother, who told the story, her family found a place where they could sharecrop with a farmer the next year. If I remember correctly, they moved close to a creek that was called Pumpkin Vine Creek.

The next year started out with good weather and the fields were put in order. Grandfather was having a hard time getting money for seed to plant. He would go into Canton to try to pick up a job that someone could pay him in money. Most of the people were like him. They had trading goods but no money. It was getting close to planting time and still no money to buy seeds. Old folks had a saying that I will always remember: "Don't worry, those who believe, God will provide."

In the meantime, something was happening at night in the house. The kids were put to bed with the understanding that they would not be wandering outside of their rooms. None of them questioned why — back then they did what they were told.

It seems that after all the kids was put to bed one night, Grandmother heard something in the hall. She got up to see what it was and found a bright light in the hall. As she moved toward it, it got brighter. It then passed her in the hall and moved though the back door, going outside. My grandmother opened the door and saw the figure going toward the springhouse. She had said two words as she passed: "silver rock." She passed into the springhouse and Grandmother went back to bed.

Most people nowadays have never heard of the silver stone. People would walk the dry creeks in the summertime, looking for rocks that were left in the creeks. The main one was the sand rock. There was a rare one that was called the silver rock. I remember as a kid seeing one in my Grandmother's house. It was made into a tabletop.

The sand rock, if buffed and polished right, looked like a desert scene. The silver rock when buffed and cleaned was like looking into a blue cloud. This one had been buffed and polished and it was a beautiful scene. I understood that my grandfather had made it into a table that you could turn over and look at the bottom. Where the bottom of the stone had lay in the creek bed, a dark crust would form. Once buffed and polished, it gave you another scene.

My mother would tell how she would sit as close to Grandfather and Grandmother as she could. She would listen to them talk about the girl that walked the hall and spoke of the silver rock. She said she had made up her mind that she would watch and see the girl in the hall.

That night, she cracked the door just enough to see the hallway. She settled in to wait. The house was quiet and everyone was supposed to be asleep. A light appeared at the end of the hallway.

I remember my mother telling how she froze where she sat by the door. She watched as the figure came down though the hall toward the back door. Then she saw her mother open the door to the room where she was and step out into the hall. She heard the figure say something as it passed through Grandmother. She said she jumped in bed and for the rest of the night her head was covered up

The next day, the family gathered together to begin the search for the silver stone.

Grandmother was determined, for she knew that somewhere close to the house there was a silver rock. The search went on for almost all of the day; no silver stone. They gave up and went to the springhouse to get a cool drink of water. Grandfather dipped a cold bucket of water from the spring and began to pass the gourd dipper around. All full of cool water, the search resumed.

Grandmother started to walk out of the springhouse when she looked down at what the bucket of water was sitting on. She moved the bucket and began to clean off the top of the rock. There, shining brightly, was the silver stone. Everyone watched as the stone was lifted up. You could hear the oohs and aahs as the stone showed what it was hiding. There, in a round circle underneath the rock, was five silver dollars.

Was this a true story? I can't say, for it happened before I was born. The old folks say it was true. If they said it was true, then we believed it.

I remember my mother talking about the good crop that they had that year. The table with the silver stone sat in my grandmother's house for years. I remember it very well. On one side of the stone it looked like beautiful blue clouds. The other side, as I remember, looked more like a face in a mist.

Lonie Adcock of Rome is a retired Rome Police Department lieutenant. His latest book is "More Memories of the Old Geezer."

GUEST COLUMN: Not if I can help it

Posted: Wednesday, September 16, 2015 6:00 am

I am sure that you have heard, or even said yourself, "They are incompetent." In some cases it is true. As we age, we get to the point to where we need someone around to keep an eye on us. You take someone who has lost a longtime mate who may seem to be in need of help. Instead of help, sometime their family will get tougher and put them in a nursing home. A nursing home in some cases is the only answer, but not in all cases.

I will try to tell this memory and stay as close to the facts as possible. I received a subpoena to be in court at an incompetency hearing. I had no idea what it was about or anything about the person listed on the subpoena. I had looked though reports and racked my brain but could not come up with anything that fit the name.

The day of the hearing I arrived early, to get some information on who and what it was all about. I tried, but could not find out anything. I took a seat

Lonie Adcock

Lonie Adcock of Rome is a retired Rome Police Department lieutenant. His latest book, "More Memories of the Old Geezer," is now available.

up front in the courtroom so I could hear as to what was going on. In a regular court the witness sits outside and is called in as needed. In an incompetency hearing the witness can sit in the courtroom

The hearing got underway and I saw a little old lady sitting in a chair with a lawyer. I had answered several calls to her house. People would pull up to the intersection and stop, then throw their garbage into her yard. I had caught several and finally got it stopped. I hadn't had a call to her house in quite a while. She sat quietly, looking straight ahead.

They began with a lawyer for the prosecutor. He went into a bunch of stuff that I thought was unnecessary. He told her age and how she wasn't responsible for her actions. He further stated she needed to be in a nursing home where she could be looked after. He kept on and on about her mental state. She sat still, not saying anything.

He sat down and the lawyer for the little old lady stood up. He hardly began to talk when I could see that he was doing her more harm than good. He rambled on about nothing that pertained to her capability of taking care of herself.

He finally sat down and the prosecutor lawyer stood up. He said he had several witness that he wanted to present.

A lady was called and he began to ask her a bunch of questions. I found out later that she was the old lady's daughter-in-law. She laid it on the old lady hard and heavy. I sat and wondered how anyone could persecute an old lady that way. Then the lawyer called a man who turned out to be her son. He did a job on his mother that I couldn't believe. He raved about her living in this big house all by herself. He stepped down and they called me to the stand.

I had no idea what they wanted from me. I sat down and looked into the face of the old lady. She gave me one of the biggest smiles that I had ever seen. Her smile seem to say to me, "It's OK, I know you have to do this."

Then it started with him wanting to know if I was familiar with the lady sitting down front at the table. I answered yes. He then wanted to know under what circumstances did I know her. I explained that I had answered several calls to her house. Then I saw what he was going to prove by my testimony. I remembered thinking, "Not if I can help it."

I said I had answered calls to her house. Then he asked me what was the circumstance of the calls. I said people were throwing paper cups and hamburger wrappers in her yard. He stopped, for I had answered in a way that he couldn't come back at me. Then he left himself wide open.

"Officer Adcock, how do you know that she didn't put that garbage in her yard trying to make you think it was some else putting it there? She could have been doing that to get attention." That was what I wanted. "She didn't put the garbage in her yard because I caught the ones who were doing it." His mouth fell open and he said, "That's all." I smiled at the old lady and took a seat.

The door of the courtroom came open with a bang and a young girl came running in. "You!" she shouted. "All of you, leave my grandmother alone." The judge banged his gavel on the desk. She paid no attention. With tears in her eyes, she ran over and hugged her grandmother. A quiet went over the courtroom. You could have heard a pin drop.

She walked over in front of the judge. As best as I can remember, she said "Your Honor, they want to take my grandmother and put her in a nursing home. They want to get her house and her money that Grandpa left her. She is capable of staying at home. I am working and taking classes but I will move in with Grandmother and look after her." Then she went over and squatted down beside her grandmother.

The judge looked around the room and, taking off his glasses, wiped his eyes. She had got to him. He put on his glasses and said to the little old lady at the table, "Why don't you come over to this chair and talk to me." He asked her questions and she answered him. For a lady her age, she was as sharp as they come. A few more question and he asked the granddaughter to come forward.

He talked to her for a while, asking her questions. The one thing he wanted to know was, would she move in with her grandmother so there would be someone around at night. She said yes and he said, "Take your grandmother and go home. You will not be bothered by anyone any more."

Court dismissed, I went out in the hallway. I was talking to someone when I felt a hand on my arm. I looked down into the face of the old lady. With a big smile she squeezed my arm and said, "Thank you, Officer Adcock. You are so nice."

I look back at the smile of the little old lady, and what she said was the reason I enjoyed being a police officer. Her people had tried to take the house that her beloved husband had built for her. Carl, as she had called him, was a carpenter and had built the house for her when they were married. She called it Carl's House.

Lonie Adcock of Rome is a retired Rome Police Department lieutenant. His latest book is "More Memories of the Old Geezer."

GUEST COLUMN: More tales from the old folks

Posted: Wednesday, September 30, 2015 6:15 am

I have been writing up some of the stories that the old folks used to tell. It was quite a treat to get to stay up late on a Saturday night and listen to the old folk stories. Most of the time we would sleep with our heads covered up the rest of the night. When the old folks told a ghost story it stayed with you.

This is one of those stories.

As I have stated before, my stories from the old folks are true but I have no way of finding out if they really happened — except take the word of the people who told them to us, our parents.

This one was supposed to have happened back in the early days of this country. There were cities, but most of the people lived in small communities.

There would be a general store, a grist mill and a blacksmith shop. As I recall, it was somewhere up in the mountains in a fertile valley called the Crossroads.

Lonie Adcock

Lonie Adcock of Rome is a retired Rome Police Department lieutenant. His latest book, "More Memories of the Old Geezer," is now available.

Saturday was the day most of the people came in to the general store and picked up what they needed for the following week. The general store housed the post office. The Saturday checkers champ was present and taking on all challengers. The young people would gather in a small park behind the store. They'd bring covered dishes and would enjoy good food and good people.

Saturdays were a time for gathering to greet your neighbors and to see if there was anything they needed. But there was one person there who cared not for his neighbors or anyone. He came to see if he could cash in on someone's misfortune.

Silas, as he was called, ran a land-buying office in the city and had several more scattered thoughout the countryside.

He was always sending out people to see if anyone was in financial trouble. It was easy to get into that position. Most people used their farm products for money. They drove to the city to the farmers market and sold their goods when the need for money arose. In the fall their cotton and corn brought in enough money to carry them through to the next season.

Everyone in the community knew Roland Smith a good, Christian, hardworking man who would give you the shirt off his back. Roland owned a section of land that was known as one of the most fertile in the community.

Silas had tried for years to get the land from Roland, with no luck. Roland seemed to prosper as Silas kept taking from people who ran into misfortune. But there comes a time in almost everyone's life when they are felled by misfortune.

An epidemic of flu went though the community and a lot of people died from it. Some of the younger ones who survived were taken with an ailment of the lungs. The only way to get over it was to go to the city and take treatments for it. This cost money and money Roland didn't have. Silas went though the community where the sickness was and started to lend money, taking land and personal things as collateral. By the time the year was over he owned almost all the land in the Crossroads valley. That is, all but Roland's section.

Then, Roland's wife, Mary, came down with the flu. It was followed by the lung disease. By then most of the money in the valley was gone and Roland could not find anyone else except Silas. Silas knew that he didn't want to put out a lot of money so he told Roland he would make him a loan on his horses. Everyone knew Roland had a pair of horses worth several times the money that Silas offered. Roland knew that he had to take it, for the sake of his wife.

Silas gave him the money with a six-month period to pay it back with interest. Otherwise, he would take the horses. And without the horses, Roland couldn't get his crop in and would have to sell his land. Silas smiled when he thought of owning the property.

Roland knew that while he was in the city with his wife that his children would keep the farm going. He bundled his wife up in the buggy and made the trip to the city. Silas would ride by Roland's farm everyday, stop and look at the crops, and smile. He tried to figure out a way to get the horses sooner, but he had to wait until the note came due.

While in the city, Roland went to see a friend who ran the local cotton gins and explained his situation. His friend took a note on his future crop of cotton and loaned him enough money to pay off Silas. When Roland came back from the city, no one knew that he carried the money to pay off his note.

After getting his wife settled in, he went down to see Silas. He arrived at the land office when Silas was out. The clerk took the money and marked the note paid in full. Roland folded the note and put it in his shirt pocket. As he walked out to the street, Silas drove up in his buggy. Not knowing that the note had been paid he greeted Roland with one of his selfish smiles. Roland greeted him and headed home.

It was said that when Silas found out Roland had paid his note he could be heard yelling all though the community.

Roland's wife got well and everything returned to normal. Roland got ready to lay out his fields for the next year. He would get out on a cool morning while the moon was still up and plow the fields. You could see him in the moonlight as you passed down the road.

Jim Miller was the local postman. He would go to the city early in the morning and pick up the mail. He would get back in time for the people to come to the general store and pick up their mail. As he passed that morning he saw Roland plowing his field. He made it back close to noon. He looked for Roland but did not see him.

Roland always pulled his wagon under a big tree close to the edge of the road. The postman drove his buggy off the road and over to the tree. There was a scene that he would never forget. Hanging from the tree with a rope around his neck was the body of Roland. Close by lay his horses shot in the heads.

Roland had been shot in the head and then hanged. Word went out in the community and no one could imagined who would do such a thing to a fine man like Roland.

The sheriff went to work on the case and soon arrested Silas. He was tried, convicted and sentence to death.

It is said that on a bright moon-lit night you can see Roland with his fine team of horses, plowing the field, getting it ready for planting. And some have said they have seen Silas lurking in the shadows, watching.

Lonie Adcock of Rome is a retired Rome Police Department lieutenant. His latest book is "More Memories of the Old Geezer."

GUEST COLUMN: Old-fashioned dentistry

Posted: Wednesday, October 14, 2015 6:15 am

I was sitting in the dentist's chair having my teeth cleaned when the lady began to talk.

I think you know how difficult it is to talk when they are scraping on your teeth. If you try to answer your tongue will get in the way, and a look will come on her face that says "be quiet." She has just asked you a question but you go and make a noise that sounds like an answer. It's hard to answer with water and a scraper and a mirror all in your mouth at the same time.

We talked about how people kept their teeth clean back when there was no money to go to a dentist. I remember how we brushed our teeth back when I was growing up. My mother would go into the woods and get a small limb from a black gum tree. She would cut it short like a tooth brush. We would chew the end of the small limb and it would become soft like a brush. She would mix salt and soda together and we would brush our teeth with it. It didn't taste good but it kept the teeth clean.

Lonie Adcock

Lonie Adcock of Rome is a retired Rome Police Department lieutenant. His latest book, "More Memories of the Old Geezer," is now available.

I heard all kinds of tales about people pulling their own teeth. I have heard of everything from pliers to vice grips being used. I bet that someone sticking a pair of vice grips into your mouth and pulling a tooth would be something. Back in my young day I can just imagine how many it would have took to hold me while some one stuck a pair of vice grips into my mouth.

I had a friend back when I was growing up that had a problem with a pair of pliers. We were in high school at the old Boys High. Our permanent teeth hadn't been with us too long. He began to have the toothache. His people, like ours, were poor and didn't have money to send him to a dentist. Every weekend the old man hit the bottle.

The boy, complaining with his tooth, went home from the park. His father, who had been on the bottle all day, made him open his mouth and he pulled the tooth with a pair of pliers. The last time

I saw him he carried a mouthful of bad teeth. The experience with the pliers held such a bad memory that he would not go to a dentist.

I remember an incident that happened back when I was getting rid of my baby teeth. It was the first one to get loose. My father wanted to pull it, but every time he tried I would holler like he was killing me. That went on for several days until the tooth was about to drop out.

My father told me to pull the tooth and put it under my pillow and the next day there would be a penny in its place for me. I walked around all day thinking about all that candy a penny would buy. That night I agreed to pull the tooth. He took a piece of sewing thread and tied it to the tooth. He opened the door and explained that he would shut the door and the tooth would be pulled. But every time he reached for the door I would holler.

He moved his chair away from the door and began to talk to me. I never noticed my sister move over to the door. My father was talking when she slammed the door shut. I looked at the string hanging from the doorknob. I reached and got it and was trying to tie the string back on my tooth. Then I saw the tooth and let out a yell that could be heard a block away.

My father calmed me down by showing me that the tooth was out. I remember that I put the tooth under my pillow that night and found a penny in its place the next morning. That was the only tooth that I ever got a penny for.

I remember another incident involving my baby teeth. My sister was five years older than me. She was a big girl, going to school, when I came up with two loose front teeth. I would catch my mother not looking and I would take my tongue and wiggle them at my sister. She would holler and my mother would take a swipe at the seat of my pants with her hand. I didn't like that but kept up the teeth-wiggling anyway.

My sister had a friend that I will call Maggie Lou. My mother told me to go and get my sister, that she was at Maggie Lou's. I went and knocked on the door. A voice said "Come in." I opened the door and stepped inside. I knew then that I had made a big mistake. My sister grabbed me and held me. I began to struggle and holler while Maggie Lou pulled my teeth. She said, "If you don't be still, I am going to kiss you." I didn't want any old girl kissing me so I held still.

I got out of there as fast as I could and went and told my mother what they had done. I opened my mouth and showed her where the teeth had been. She started to laugh and I went out on the front porch and sat down. I don't recall wiggling any more teeth at anyone, especially my sister.

Once I got a call at the police department to a house where a fight was going on. I walked up to the front door and an elderly man met me there. He invited me in. An old lady sat in front of the television. He told me to overlook her, she wasn't important. He sat down and began to talk. Than he pointed — "The woman is the problem. She knocked out my teeth and now I can't eat my supper."

I looked him over but didn't see any blood on him. He kept on talking, telling me about her and his teeth. I stopped him and asked, "Where are your teeth if she knocked them out?" He got up and went into the kitchen. He held a plate to where I could see it. There was a set of broken false teeth on it. I started to leave and the old lady stood up. Looking me square in the face, she said, "Hit the road, Buster, before you will have to tangle with me."

I remember laughing about it later. Here stood a woman well in her 70s, about 5 feet tall, weighing no more than 100 pounds telling a 6-foot, 190-pound man that he didn't want to tangle with her. I remember looking her in the face and saying "Lady, I sure don't want to tangle with anyone as mean as you." I closed the door very gently as I left.

Lonie Adcock of Rome is a retired Rome Police Department lieutenant. His latest book is "More Memories of the Old Geezer."

GUEST COLUMN: Lullaby: A life well-spent

Posted: Wednesday, October 28, 2015 6:15 am

It was said about him that even if he was taking a shower or cleaning a horse stable, he had a smile on his face and a song on his lips.

I don't ever recall seeing him without the smile and a song. I was a small child when he was around.

We lived at the end of the old Hardin Bridge. My father was farming and Lullaby worked for the people that owned the land. He was what was called a handyman around the farm. Thinking back, he couldn't have been much over 20 years old.

I recall hearing the people who lived and worked the land talk about him. They said he came to the farm and got a job at an early stage in life. He made a good worker so the owner of the farm kept him on. There did not seem to be anything that he couldn't do. Most people who knew him liked his smile and singing most of all. He was liked by all that knew him and came in contact with him.

Lonie Adcock

Lonie Adcock of Rome is a retired Rome Police Department lieutenant. His latest book, "More Memories of the Old Geezer," is now available.

The first time that I can recall seeing him was at an all-day singing and dinner on the ground at the church.

He was busy helping with the setting-up of the tables. When he was no longer needed, he got his guitar and sat down, leaning back against a tree. He began to pick and sing. I moved in as close to him as I could. I remember he sang nothing but church songs. The one that stayed with me down though the years was "Church in the Wildwood."

That was when I first noticed how gently he handled the old beat-up guitar. You would have thought it was a small baby. He sang at all church functions if he was asked. Mothers looked at him, wishing they had a son like him. Men admired him for the young man he was; the girls all looked at him with that look in their eyes and a sigh.

On Saturday the man who owned the farm would let him have the cotton truck and he would go around and pick up the people who lived on the farm and take them to Kingston. It was always a treat to get to ride up front with him. He would talk but most of the time he was singing.

On this Saturday we were crossing the bridge when we saw a family stranded on the side of the road. Lullaby stopped to see if he could help them. The lady and two children came over to the truck. She stated that they were trying to get home. It seemed that they had been to visit some kinfolks when their car had broke down. Her husband had gone to try to find someone to come back and get them.

Lullaby got out and asked them to get up on the truck. We hadn't gone far until we saw a man walking on the side of the road. Lullaby stopped and found he was the woman's husband. He got on the truck and Lullaby started for Kingston. When we got to Kingston we found that the people lived several miles from Kingston. Lullaby unloaded everyone then took the family home. He drove back and parked in the park where we all knew he would be.

This is another story that was told about him:

It seems that the preacher's car broke down and had to be left at the church. Lullaby had a big Packard then. They said he kept it shined up and called it his courting car. I remember him taking me over to Euharlee and buying me a stick of peppermint candy. I thought I was something, sitting in that big shiny car.

It was said that the preacher had a seminar in Atlanta but, with his car broke down, had no way of getting there. He was supposed to leave on Sunday evening and go to Atlanta.

That morning, Lullaby drove his courting car to church and handed the keys to the preacher. At first the preacher refused to take the keys. They said Lullaby smiled at him and said, "Preacher, you play around with my soul — why won't you drive my car? Is my car more precious than my soul?" He smiled as the preacher took the keys, then he took a seat with the other people in the church. The preacher brought back the car with a new wax job and a tank full of gas.

There was an incident where he was picking and singing in the park at Kingston. The sheriff came up and decided to have some fun. He told Lullaby that if he didn't play "Barbara Allen" he was going to take him to jail for playing in public without a license. When Lullaby got through with "Barbara Allen," the sheriff told him he could play anywhere he wanted to.

I don't recall anyone ever saying anything bad about him. If you needed help, he was always ready to lend a hand. We moved from the old Hardin Bridge while I was still a small kid. I will always remember him. I heard several stories as to what happened to him later on.

There's another story that has stayed with me when I think of the man called Lullaby. (It seems that no one really knew his name. When asked his name, he would just say Lullaby.)

It was told that when World War II started he joined the Army. When the beach at Normandy was stormed he was driving a landing barge. He had unloaded and started back for another load when a mortar shell hit his barge.

It was my understanding he was buried overseas. I used to think what a sad ending for such a good man. I now realize that he was needed in heaven so God sent for him.

Lonie Adcock of Rome is a retired Rome Police Department lieutenant. His latest book is "More Memories of the Old Geezer."

GUEST COLUMN: Making friends in Hell's Hollow

Posted: Wednesday, November 11, 2015 6:00 am

Having grown up around Rome, I look back at places that used to be but no longer exist.

There in Anchor Duck were some houses between the railroad tracks that was called Snake Island. Scant Corners was at Martha Berry and West Tenth. You can see the name but oldtimers will tell you that the Scant Corners we knew no longer exists. A Saturday night on Scant Corners was something to remember.

There is one place that was going strong when I was growing up, that if you speak of it they will look at you kind of funny. Most people nowadays have never heard of a place called Hell's Hollow. Most of the people will shake their head and say "Hell's Hollow? Never heard of such a place. Where was it?"

It was in the area just below the Civic Center. The first time that I ever saw it, it was full of run-down houses. It was a place where poor folk lived. It was

Lonie Adcock

Lonie Adcock of Rome is a retired Rome Police Department lieutenant. His latest book, "More Memories of the Old Geezer," is now available.

a place where you could pick up a pint of white whiskey. I knew two bootleggers that lived in Hell's Hollow. I bet you are wondering, that far back, how a small boy could know bootleggers.

When school was out on Friday, I would hurry home. Back then you had what was called school clothes and everyday clothes. When school was out you hurried home and changed clothes as fast as possible. On Fridays I would grab my fishing pole and head for the river. I would catch enough fish to sell and make what we called show fare, to see Gene Autry and Roy Rogers at the movies.

To get to what I called my catfish hole, I would come off Fifth Avenue at the end of the bridge and come down by the old jail. There were houses all though the area. The road that led to Celanese was not much more than a road of potholes. I would go down by where the library is now. There were houses on both sides of the road. There was a cemetery on the right side of the road. And there was one house that sat down in a field on the side where the river ran. I would go down by the house to get on the riverbank.

I had been down to my favorite spot and had caught a good-size string of catfish. I made it to the road and was resting when a gentleman came by. He stopped and looked at my fish.

"What are you going to do with all the fish?" he asked. "I am going to sell them," I said. I could tell by the look in his eyes that he wanted them. "What will you give me for them?" I asked. He scratched his head saying, "Mighty fine-looking fish." I watched him trying to put a price on them. I knew about what I had been getting for them from the people up on the hill behind Broad Street. "If you will come with me, I will give you two dollars for half of them." He said. "A friend of mine will give you two dollars and a half for the others."

This was the best offer I had ever had. I followed him as he crossed the road and started toward the Civic Center. I had never been in the Hollow so I was surprised at what I saw.

He said his name was Foster. He was a tall lanky fellow and one of his steps made about five of mine. I was trying to keep up, but carrying the string of fish and my fishing pole was too much. He stopped, smiling. He handed me the brown paper sack that he carried and took my fish. The sack he gave me to carry felt like it was empty compared with the fish.

We came to the Hollow and he went up the steps to the first house. I will always remember what he did as I stepped upon the porch. He opened the door and to someone inside said, "Alright, you in there. Keep your language decent. I have a young gentleman with me and he doesn't need to hear your mouth."

I followed him into the kitchen where a lady was cooking. She made a fuss about the fish and, when I started out the door to the porch, handed me another dollar. Foster came out carrying about half of the fish and said, "Come on. We will sell the rest to my friend Rooster." I remember thinking what man had a rooster for a friend — specially one who ate catfish.

I followed him down the step and across the road to a house. He knocked on the door and yelled as loud as he could, "Rooster, get your big self out here." I got myself into position to see him, and I did. The biggest man I believe that I had ever seen came through the door. He had to turn sideways in order to get though the door.

I backed to the edge of the porch to where I could run if he got after me. He had a big smile on his face and I knew that he wasn't going to hurt me. Foster held up the fish, showing them to him. They were still flopping around on the stringer. Foster asked, "What about it, Rooster? A mess of fresh catfish for three dollars." I didn't say anything. I watched Rooster. I could tell he was going to buy them but wanted to haggle. He and Foster began to haggle over the price. Foster wound up getting me six dollars for all of them.

With money in my pocket I left, promising them that I would bring them some more the next weekend. I remember Foster telling me to never come in the Hollow after dark. He said it "wasn't no place for a small gentleman." I was told to always come to his house first. I met a lady who lived there named Edna. Edna was a nice lady who always had a piece of cake for a small starving boy.

I made some friends in Hell's Hollow but never went there after dark. I know now that Foster and Rooster were selling white whiskey. I saw the police raid them several time while I was selling my fish. We moved from Fourth Ward and I lost sight of the people who had been friends to a small boy. I often wonder what happened to them.

Lonie Adcock of Rome is a retired Rome Police Department lieutenant. His latest book is "More Memories of the Old Geezer."

GUEST COLUMN: Just an old-fashioned hayride

Posted: Wednesday, November 25, 2015 6:15 am

How many people, I wonder, have ever been on an old-fashioned hayride? I am talking of a hayride on an old wagon, loaded with hay, pulled by a pair of mules. Sometimes there would be people with guitars playing music. The crowd would sing and a good time was had by all.

It was one of them Saturday nights with a short payday. Duke and I were sitting in the park trying to figure out what we were going to do. A crowd began to gather and we joined them. We were talking about it being a Saturday night and no place to go. Then, from out of nowhere, the conversation turned to a hayride.

I had never been on a hayride, nor had some of the others. One of the people in the park said they knew where a Saturday night hayride was held. After we decided that the people would all pay their own way, we loaded up Duke's Hudson with girls and headed to the hay ride

Lonie Adcock

Lonie Adcock of Rome is a retired Rome Police Department lieutenant. His latest book, "More Memories of the Old Geezer," is now available.

We headed for a farm on the Black's Bluff Road. We arrived to see a large crowd gathered. We got out and a man dressed in overalls came over to us. He told us that the ride would cost us 50 cents apiece. We bought our tickets and he led us over to a wagon loaded with hay. He told us to hold on to our tickets for there would be a drawing for a prize later on. The winner would win two free rides for the following Saturday night.

I crawled up on the hay and found a good place. Our crowd all gathered together and began to talk. I was surprised for it wasn't too long before the wagon was loaded. They brought out several mules and hitched them to the wagon. A place beside the driver was where the man with the guitar sat. The driver gave us a talk, telling us that we would not be permitted to jump off the wagon while it was moving. Making sure that everyone understood the rules, he headed the wagon out onto the road.

Those of you who travel the Bluff Road know what it looks like today. If you knew the road back in the '40s, you would not believe it. There was this farm and a few houses scattered along the road. We pulled out into the road and the man with the guitar began to sing, "She be coming around the mountain." I think everyone on the wagon was singing and whipping it up.

We came to what was called the Chain Gang Camp at that time. I think it has another name now. The driver stopped the wagon so we could get a good look at the camp. Then he gave us a talk about what would put us in there. When he got though and the wagon began to move, everyone was so quiet that a cough from someone startled the crowd. Then the guitar started back and we all began to sing again.

We went past the Chain Gang Camp and it was beginning to get dark. We pulled in to an area and they turned the wagon around. What I didn't understand was why they began to light lanterns that hung around on the wagon. It was a bright moonlit night and we didn't need light. The driver explained that was so a car could see us and not run into the wagon. As I recall, we had not seen a car since we left the farm.

By the time we got back to the Chain Gang Camp no one saw it, for they all had snuggled down into the hay and had something else on their minds. We came back to a road that run from the Bluff Road to what was Highway 27. It came out just below Darlington School. I believe at that time it was called Park Road.

We went up the road for a short piece, then the driver turned the wagon off the road and into a dirt road. The dirt road ran along beside the other road then took a right turn and headed uphill. I often wondered how those two mules pulled that wagon and its load.

Then the wagon came to a halt under a big oak tree. We were told to get off and to gather around him. I got off and walked over to the tree. I had the oddest feeling when I got off the wagon. The driver motioned me to come back. We stood around him and I have never felt so uneasy in a place in all my life.

It was a hot night but I had chills all over me. The hair stood up on the back of my neck. I didn't know anything about the place where we were, but I knew he was going to tell us a ghost story.

The crowd was quiet; no one spoke. He started telling his story. I never really knew if it was true or just a story that he told for our benefit. I went back later and I believe his story. It went like this:

On a clear moonlit night you could see a spirit moving around under the big oak tree. Many years back a woman had come up missing in the area. A search party was formed and she was found. He pointed to the big oak tree and said "The tree was much smaller at the time. She was killed and her body tied to the tree. She had been there for several days before being found."

The story went on to say that a prisoner from the Chain Gang Camp had escaped and killed her. He was caught and paid for his crime. I watched the driver go over to the tree and put his hand on it. "Does anyone wish to touch the tree were the woman's body was found?" I walked over to where he stood. He gave me a strange look and said, "Here." I reached out and put my hand against the tree.

Then I got back on the wagon and sat down and the rest of them began to load up. As the wagon moved back down the hill toward the road, I knew that I would be back and check out this place.

We moved back out into the road and went toward Highway 27. A short time and we pulled into a yard that had some fires going in the backyard. We were told to unload and to grab us something to eat. A table full of hot dogs and potato chips awaited. I sat down at the end of the table and began to eat.

Francis, a girl that was with us, sat down beside me. I watched her, knowing that she had something on her mind. I smiled and said, "Speak up. I know what you got on your mind." She asked, "Are we coming back to that big oak tree?" "As soon as we can," I answered. Duke and the others came over to where Francis and I sat. The guitar man began to play and everyone ate and sang. Everyone forget about the oak tree but Francis and me.

We loaded up for the trip back to the farm on Bluff Road. As we passed the big oak tree, I felt Francis squeeze my arm. She was pointing toward it. I saw what she saw but marked it off to the way the moonlight was hitting the area.

Once all the girls were unloaded, Duke drove me home. We talked about the oak tree and paying it a visit real soon.

Lonie Adcock of Rome is a retired Rome Police Department lieutenant. His latest book is "More Memories of the Old Geezer."

GUEST COLUMN: Don't forget me, Mister

Posted: Wednesday, December 9, 2015 6:15 am

I've heard of people who could forget bad memories by removing them from their mind. I choose to keep all my memories, good or bad.

Once I was promoted to the rank of detective sergeant I was placed in the plainclothes division, the 5 p.m. to 1 a.m. shift. This shift dealt with a lot of shoplifting cases.

This particular incident involved a call to a grocery store to pick up a shoplifter. I remember it as if it happened yesterday.

I responded to the call and when I arrived at the store, I was told they were holding the suspect in the manager's office. As I approached the office, I saw a little old lady standing in front of a rack of cakes. She appeared to be eating one of the cakes. As I approached the two men who were standing there with her, one of them walked off.

"You call the police?" I asked the one remaining.

Lonie Adcock

Lonie Adcock of Rome is a retired Rome Police Department lieutenant. His latest book, "More Memories of the Old Geezer," is now available.

He pointed to the little old lady. "Take her and charge her with shoplifting."

I looked at the little old lady and I knew he could see the disbelief on my face. She had to be at least 80 years old and couldn't have weighed more than 75 pounds. I watched as she ate the cake she had taken from the rack.

Turning to the clerk, I asked, "Are you going to prosecute this old lady?"

"Yes" he replied "The manager wants her put in jail for shoplifting."

"Look at her," I said. "Shes no thief. She's an old lady who's hungry."

"I know, but I have to do what the manager says."

"Where's the manager?"

The clerk pointed toward a closed door. I headed that way. The clerk called after me, "He doesn't want to talk to you."

I know I replied, "Tough. He will talk to me."

I tried to open the door, but it was locked. I knocked and a girl opened it.

"I want to talk to the store manager," I told her.

She opened the door and I walked into the office. The manager sat behind the desk with a frown on his face. He made it quite plain that he didn't want to talk to me. I walked into the office. Taking a chair that was in front of his desk, I plopped it down next to him. He had to swivel to look at me.

"What can I do for you, Detective?" he asked.

"We need to talk about that old lady you have out there."

"I want her prosecuted for shoplifting."

"I can't put her in jail for shoplifting," I replied.

He smirked and said, "And tell me why not?"

"She has done no shoplifting."

"She took a cake from the rack and ate it," the manager exclaimed.

"That is theft, not shoplifting."

We sat there a good 30 minutes, arguing back and forth. I finally got him to agree to let me pay for the cake and promise that she would not come back into his store. I put the little old lady in the car with the understanding that there would be no prosecuting for her eating the cake.

On the way to the station, I stopped and picked up a hamburger and some fries. When we arrived, I took her to our breakroom, bought her a Coke and sat her down to eat.

A female dispatcher was on duty and I explained to her what was going on. I asked her to meet with the old lady and try to find out her name and where she lived. Meanwhile, I called family services and explained the situation. The lady from family services said she was not familiar with her, but she would call some of the caseworkers to try to find someone who was.

Then I went back to the breakroom to see if the dispatcher had found out anything. She explained that the old lady didn't know what her name was or where she lived.

The other dispatcher came to the door and told me I had a call from family services. I picked up the telephone and the lady explained that she was familiar with the case and told me to meet her on First Avenue. That was apparently where the old lady lived.

I took the lady to the address on First Avenue. The caseworker was waiting for us. She explained that the old lady lived by herself but recently she had begun to develop dementia. The only known relative, a son, lived somewhere in Tennessee. She said she had a telephone number and would get in touch with him tomorrow.

She wanted me to go in the house with her and look around. The door was unlocked and the lights were on, so we went inside. I noticed that the mailbox was stuffed full of mail, so I took the stack and placed it on a table in the living room.

There were several checks in the stack of mail but there was no food in the house. I often wondered how long that old lady had gone without food before eating the cake at the store.

The caseworker said she would take the lady to a safe place, where she would receive care until her son could be notified. We found a key for the house, locked up and went to the street where the lady was waiting. I tried to escort her to the caseworker's car but she pulled back and headed over to my car.

I explained to her that she would have to go with the caseworker. Up to then she hadn't spoke a word to me. She mumbled something that I didn't catch, but have wondered about all these years.

The next day when I arrive at work I had a message to call the lady from family services, who told me the son had come down taken her back to Tennessee. It was good to hear that the little old lady had been taken care of. I hoped that I would never run across a case like that again.

Those words she mumbled to me sure did sound like "Don't forget me, Mister."

Lonie Adcock of Rome is a retired Rome Police Department lieutenant. He is the author of "More Memories of the Old Geezer" and is preparing to release "Fact or Fiction."

GUEST COLUMN: Looking for his Angel at Fourth and Broad

Posted: Wednesday, December 23, 2015 6:45 am

Now that I am growing older and becoming an old geezer, I think a lot about things that happened in the past. Some memories are of the good times and some are of the bad. Sometimes bad memories are forgotten and sometimes they aren't. This particular incident I'm writing about happened many years ago and has become one of my cherished memories.

I had worked a burglary in South Rome when I noticed my watch had stopped. There was a watch repair shop at the corner of Fourth Avenue and Broad Street so I dropped by. The owner of the shop was standing out front when I arrived.

He spoke as I walked up.

"Good morning, Officer Adcock."

"Morning, Gene," I answered. "I need you to take a look at this piece of junk," I said, as I handed him my watch.

Lonie Adcock

Lonie Adcock of Rome is a retired Rome Police Department lieutenant. His latest book, "More Memories of the Old Geezer," is now available.

He took it and laughed. "Did you shake it?" Then he started to walk toward the corner of Fourth Avenue. "I want to show you something."

I followed him to the corner where he pointed to an old fellow sitting on a bench across the street.

"Watch him," he said.

I watched the old man as he leaned forward and held still for a few minutes. Then he would lean back. He held a walking stick and would use it as a prop — leaning forward, then back. We both watched as he rocked back and forth.

"He comes to town about twice a week and sits on the bench. I've watched him before," Gene said. "Why don't you go and talk to him while I check your watch. He sits there for about an hour then gets up and goes up the street. I watch him as he turns down Fifth Avenue."

"Sure, why not," I answered.

I started across the street, watching the old fellow rock back and forth. I approached the bench and he leaned forward, not realizing I was there. He was talking to himself. I stood by quietly and heard the word "Angel."

When he grew quiet, I spoke. "Sir," I said. "Are you all right?" At that he looked up and smiled.

"Oh yes, Officer. I am quite all right." He moved over on the bench. "Have a seat and we will talk."

I sat down and waited for him to say something.

"I bet you are wondering what an old man is doing sitting on a bench on Broad Street in the hot sunshine."

I didn't reply because I could tell he was ready to talk.

"Look up the street, Officer, and tell me what you see."

I looked up the street and saw cars and people.

"What do you see, Officer?"

"I see cars and people," I answered.

He grew silent as I waited. Then he said, "Let me tell you what I see when I look up the street. I see my Angel, and she is just as pretty today as she was then."

He paused, then continued softly.

"I was in the Army when I first saw my Angel. It was here on this corner. I had started across the street when a siren began to go off. The street was cleared and from up the street came the sound of music. I stepped out into the street to see what was happening.

"There, coming down the street, was a marching band. And out in front of the band were three majorettes, and out in front of them was my Angel. She was the prettiest girl I have ever seen. I watched as she approached the intersection. She stopped in front of me and winked.

"In those days, girls didn't wink at boys. I just stood there as she went marching on down the street. I knew that the girl I was going to marry had just winked at me. I wasted no time in getting over to the football game. We met, courted and was married."

He grew silent. I waited until he turned back to me with tears in his eyes.

"My Angel got sick; the doctor said she had cancer. After that, it was in and out of the hospital. Finally, I carried her on what I knew was the time we had been dreading. I was sitting by the side of her bed, holding her hand. I felt a slight squeeze and she opened her eyes. I bent over and kissed her forehead and she smiled and winked. I felt her hand go limp and I knew that my Angel was gone."

I watched the tears run down his cheek as I stood up. He leaned forward looking up the street and I turned and walked away.

He no longer knew I was there, for he was watching his Angel come marching down the street. Catching the light, I crossed the street and headed for the watch repair shop. My watch just needed a battery. I checked back into service and pulled away, taking a last look at the old man sitting on the bench.

As I turned up Fourth Avenue I said to myself, "Girls didn't wink at boys back in those days, but Angels did."

Lonie Adcock of Rome is a retired Rome Police Department lieutenant. His latest book is "More Memories of the Old Geezer."

GUEST COLUMN: Buddy: A story of babies

Posted: Wednesday, January 6, 2016 6:00 am

I was thinking about an incident that happened during my days on the Rome Police Department. I was given an address and was told that an officer needed to see me. The officer was standing on the porch with a lady. As I approached, I could see that she was crying. I noticed that something was covered up, lying on the steps. The officer came to meet me.

He started to tell me about the problem. The lady had a small dog that she called Buddy. Buddy was a rat terrier. He shook his head and said, "Lieutenant, I will let her tell you what happened."

I walked over to where the dog lay, covered up. I pulled back the cover to see what had happened. There was blood all over the dog's head. I could see that it had been shot with a small caliber rifle. I walked up on the porch where the woman sat crying and sat down in a chair beside her. She looked up at me with the most awful look that I have ever seen.

Lonie Adcock

Lonie Adcock of Rome is a retired Rome Police Department lieutenant. His latest book, "More Memories of the Old Geezer," is now available.

She reached out her hand and I took it in mine. "You feel like telling me what happened?" I asked. She stopped crying and I waited for her to speak. In a class at the police academy I learned that if someone is crying, sometimes a touch will calm her down. It said a hug would do it but if you couldn't hug them, take their hand and hold it. As a police officer I couldn't go around hugging people, but I could take their hand. I had never tried it before but it seemed to work. She wiped her eyes, looked at me and began to talk.

She said that Buddy stayed inside at night but he stayed outside during the day. Her place was fenced in so Buddy could only stay in her yard. She had let him out that morning and walked down to a store on Maple Street. On her way back she had heard what sounded like a gunshot. She got home and found Buddy dead on the steps. She had called the police and sat down on the porch and cried.

I let go of her hand and, turning to the officer, said "Let's take a walk." We walked around behind the house, to the edge of the fence. There in the back yard stood a boy with a rifle in his hands. He never saw me. I saw blood where the dog had been shot. The fence had a sag in it as if some one had crawled over it.

I called headquarters on my walkie talkie, telling them what I had. It wasn't just a few minutes before a car pulled up in front of the house where the boy was. I watched him hide the rifle and go meet the officers. He was laughing and talking as if he had not done anything. I called the officer and told them where the rifle was. They got the rifle and brought him around to where I was.

I watched as the officers got the boy out of the car. He was a big boy for his age. He came over and, looking at the wrapped-up dog, he smiled. I knew we had our shooter. I took him by the shoulder, letting my fingers dig in. No one could see what I was doing. It looked as if I was standing with my hands on his shoulder.

"Why," I asked "did you shoot this lady's dog?" I let up and stepped back. He again put a smirk on his face. His words as I remember: "I don't like animals, that why." I told the officer to take him to the station and book him. He began to laugh.

"What's so funny?" I asked. He said, "I will be out before dark for I am a juvenile. I am only 16." I walked over to the lady and asked her was there any thing we could do for her. She then surprised me and the officer with me. "Yes," she said. "Will you help me bury Buddy?" We were on duty but there was no way that we could refuse. We buried Buddy close to a big rose bush in the back yard. That was the first and only time I ever did anything like that.

This should be the end of the story — with the shooter in custody and Buddy buried — but I feel compelled to write about the boy who shot Buddy. His name was Melvin and he was, as he said, 16 years old.

The next day, I rode down the street where he lived. He was sitting on his front porch. As I approached he stood up, bowing and waving, making sure that I saw him. He held up his wrist to show that he did not have handcuffs on. I smiled to myself and said, "Carry on, my day will come."

Then a series of burglaries started in the Maple Street area. It was the kind that mostly took money. Some burglars only took money because it could not be traced. This went on for quite a while. Then one night a patrol officer caught Melvin in a store. He spent time in a juvenile facility but was soon out again. This went on for some time. They would catch him and he would go off for a while. Whether he was out of town on his own or through the court, I never found out.

One day, I was turning around in the parking lot of what was at that time the Maple on the Hill when a car went by with something sticking out the windows. I pulled out behind it and turned on my blue light. He pulled over and I slowly walked up to where I could see in the car. There were two people in the car. The driver was Melvin.

As he was getting out, a patrol car pulled in with me and the officer got the passenger out too. I reached though and got the keys out of the car. I told the officer to check to see what they had in the car. He came back to me shaking his head. "Lieutenant, you are not going to believe what that is sticking out the window." We put the two in cuffs and placed them in a caged car. Then I asked the officer what he found. "Lieutenant, you will not believe it. It's a back seat of marijuana," he said.

I looked and, sure enough, the stuff sticking out the window was marijuana. I went back to the patrol car. Opening the door I asked, "Where did you get the weed?" He laughed real loud. "That came from my private field." I knew that I wasn't going to find out anything. I would turn him over to the drug people.

I had his license in my hand when he laughed again, saying "I will be out before you come back to work." He was still relying on being a juvenile. I turned the light on the license to where I could get a good look. I smiled. "One more question before we go to headquarters and book you," I said. "What is your birth date?" A funny look came on his face. I knew that he had remembered that this was his 18th birthday. He was no longer a juvenile. I laughed and said "You are no longer a juvenile; you belong to me." I shut the car door and told the officer to take him to the station.

As I remember, he served time and when he got out he moved to Macon. We all said good riddance when we found he had gone to another town.

I would ride down the street where little Buddy was killed. The lady would be sitting on the porch by herself. She had said that she would never have another animal of any kind. When I asked her why, she had said, "because Buddy was my baby."

Lonie Adcock of Rome is a retired Rome Police Department lieutenant. His latest book is "More Memories of the Old Geezer."

Sponsored From Around the Web

GUEST COLUMN: Cathead biscuits, bucksop gravy and some other hard times food

Posted: Wednesday, January 20, 2016 6:00 am

When I was growing up in the 1930s, times were hard. It wasn't much better in the '40s. If you had a job back then, you were lucky.

I had to go to work at the ripe old age of 13. My first full-time job was as a dishwasher in a cafe. I graduated from dishwasher to assistant cook. It was there that I learned there were other foods besides beans, taters and cornbread.

Don't get me wrong. To a hungry boy, beans and taters with a big piece of onion was awfully good. There were times when there was no beans and taters on the table.

Let's look at some of the food and what it was called.

If you wanted some bread but didn't have the flour to make biscuits, there was a hoecake. You made your dough up real thin. Then you poured a thin layer in an iron skillet on top of an eye of the stove. The hoecake would brown on one side then you would flip it over.

Lonie Adcock

Lonie Adcock of Rome is a retired Rome Police Department lieutenant. His latest book, "More Memories of the Old Geezer," is now available.

In later years I heard it called fry bread. I grew up eating a lot of hoecake bread. Don't get the fry bread mixed up with flapjacks.

When I talk about flapjacks, you think of pancakes, but flapjacks was the poor folks' version of pancakes. There was some other things put in the mixture for flapjacks that was not in hoecakes.

Making hoecake bread, you poured the whole bottom of the frying pan full. For flapjacks, you put small portions of the mixture in the pan. There would be about four in the pan at the same time.

A stack of them with good cow butter in between and sorghum syrup poured on top — this would fill the stomach of a poor boy and keep him going until bean time.

Bean time was at the time most folks call lunch. It was cooked and ready, but most of the time the husband was off working and the kids were in school. The beans were held over for dinner, what was known as supper time back then. The whole family sat down and ate together. If you were lucky, you had beans and taters with an onion and cornbread. Everyone ate the same thing, with no complaints.

I guess you noticed I spelled potatoes as "taters." When we were growing up, our mother would give us a few cents and tell us to run to the store and get some taters. The taters would be in a box in the store. You could pick out the ones you wanted. If you picked them out you had no complaint if one was bad.

I can remember when a 25-cent piece would buy a big bag of taters.

Nowadays they would not even let you smell of a tater for a quarter.

There were all kind of beans back then. Pinto and butter beans were the most popular. In case you didn't know, the big lima bean was called butter bean. Among the other favorite was the black-eyed peas. Leftovers were put into the icebox and warmed up the next day. The black-eyed peas were different.

If you had black-eyed peas for supper, you could bet that you would have pea patties for breakfast. The peas were mashed and an egg was broke into them with salt and pepper to season. Flour was mixed into the pea mixture and made into patties. They were fried into a crispy patty.

The pea patty with some eggs and a cathead biscuit made a breakfast fit for a poor boy.

I bet you are saying to yourself, "What in world is a cathead biscuit?" I can remember when it was the thing to have hot biscuits for breakfast.

Mothers thought you had to have a good breakfast in order for you to be healthy.

Biscuits came in all sizes. Some small, some medium, and the big cathead biscuit. If your mother made the small biscuit, it took a lot of them to fill a hungry person. The medium was a little better. The big cathead biscuit only took about one, two at the most. You take and split the biscuit and fill it full of good old country butter. If you have gravy, pour it over the biscuit.

Did I mention gravy? There was several kinds of gravy back then. I remember redeye gravy. Then there was sawmill gravy. And don't leave out bucksop gravy.

Redeye gravy you got from frying some kind of meat. I remember that the old folks would pour a small amount of coffee into the grease. They would mix it real good and pour it over all kind of greens. If you had no milk or anything but flour, you would make bucksop gravy with water. It looked like gravy but didn't have the taste of sawmill gravy. Sawmill gravy was made with milk and if you were lucky, you had sausage to put into it. The gravy without anything in it was great on a big cathead biscuit. The sausage would make it lip-smacking good.

Did I say lip-smacking good? Well now, if you have never had old-fashioned cold bread pudding, you don't know what you have missed.

The leftover bread was kept and, when there was enough, my mother would make it into cold bread pudding.

I have no way of knowing what was put in the cold bread or how it was made, but after you had your beans and taters a slice of cold bread pudding set off the supper. It was lip-smacking good.

If you were lucky, your mother had enough stuff in the kitchen to make up a batch of tea cakes.

I have ate all kinds of cookies, but none can come up to the home-cooked tea cake.

I have talked about beans, gravy, and a few other things. There was then, and now, nothing as good as a made-from-scratch chocolate or coconut cake.

I have always credited a lot of the taste of the food back then to the old wood stove. A biscuit baked in the oven had a taste that you can't find nowadays.

The cathead biscuits are still found in several places. They are good, but Mama's good old cathead biscuits were the best. Did I mention, to make this taste real good you had a big cup of joe with it?

Lonie Adcock of Rome is a retired Rome Police Department lieutenant. His latest book is "More Memories of the Old Geezer."

GUEST COLUMN: Snakes and skinny dips in the old swim hole

Posted: Wednesday, February 3, 2016 6:00 am

I am sure that back in the old days most people had a favorite place to go swimming on a hot day. Some were fortunate enough to have a good clear lake; most of us had a wide place in a creek.

One of my favorite places was Dykes Creek. You could go in Dykes Creek in the middle of July and when you hit the water you would think there was ice in there. The water coming from the spring kept the water cold, winter or summer.

My mother was very strict about me getting into a creek. I remember she told me never to go in water until I learned how to swim. I would ask her, "How am I going to learn how to swim if I don't get into the water?" She would shake her head and say, "Young man, you hear me. Don't let me catch you in a creek."

Like all boys, I didn't hear her — and every chance I got, I went into the creek. Needless to say at my ripe old age, I never learned how to swim.

Lonie Adcock

Lonie Adcock of Rome is a retired Rome Police Department lieutenant. His latest book, "More Memories of the Old Geezer," is now available.

I remember one Sunday that Duke and I decided to go to Dykes Creek and go swimming. It was one of those hot days when a dip in the cold water felt good.

At the intersection of Kingston and Calhoun Avenue a man was selling watermelons from the back of a truck. We pulled in and talked to the man with the watermelons for a while. We talked him down to 25 cents apiece for the melons. We put four in the trunk of the car and headed for the creek.

When we got to the creek we found that it was crowded with people. Some we knew and some we didn't.

We found a place to park and began to look for a place to put our watermelons in the creek. We put pieces of dead wood in a circle and put the watermelons in the middle of them. Making sure that they would stay in place and not float away, we jumped in the creek. I remember that when you first hit the water you felt like you were in a pond of ice water.

After a while in the water, we decided to cut one of the watermelons. It was good and cold. The creek had kept it cold like a refrigerator would. We ate it and then got back into the water. It kept getting hotter and hotter.

Some of the people from the park had come up so we decided to cut another watermelon. One of the girls said she would go and get the watermelon out of the creek. We fixed up a place where we could slice it into pieces. With everything ready, we waited for the watermelon. Then I saw the girl who went to get it standing on the bank staring into the water.

I walked over and looked at the water to see what she was staring at. There, lying on one of the watermelons, was the biggest snake that I had ever seen. He was lying on the watermelon curled up. I motioned and told her to go get us a watermelon. She looked at me and said, "You want a watermelon, you go and get it."

She called and the others came over to see what was the holdup. It seemed that no one wanted watermelon bad enough to go and get one. Laughing, I picked up a rock and threw it at the snake. I hit him and he fell off into the water. I watched, thinking he would go away. He turned and headed toward the bank where I was.

I ran and jumped up on the fender of a car. He kept on coming. Everybody scattered, some getting on the car and some getting in their cars. I watched him as he moved around among the cars. He finally decided it was too hot so he headed back toward the water. I watched as he went into the water. I picked up several big sized rocks. I did not intend for him to have my watermelons.

He went into the water and shimmed back to the watermelons. He crawled back up on the watermelons and curled up. I knew if I threw a rock and it hit one of the watermelons that it would burst. It was easy to see that the snake had settled down and did not intend to leave. I motioned for the people to get back and get ready to run.

I got into a good position and let a rock fly. It was a round sand rock. A round sand rock was the best kind to throw.

The rock hit his head and he went into the water. He hit the water rolling and curling. I let go with a second rock. I will never understand how it happened, but just as he rolled with his mouth open the rock hit him in the head. I could tell that he would not bother us anymore for he began to float away.

I walked the bank of the creek for apiece, making sure that he did not come back. I waded out and got the watermelons. I will never forget how that snake came after us. I can't recall ever seeing another snake in Dykes Creek.

It was a cool night and we had loaded the car down with people and went to the Drive In. Back then they had a carload for $1 night. After the movie, the subject of skinny dipping came up. They began to dare each other, saying they were scared to go skinny dipping at night.

Now this is somewhere around 11 o'clock at night. We headed for Dykes Creek to see how many would jump into the icy water. When we arrived the door opened and, to my surprise, clothes began to come off and people hit the icy water. I sat down on the fender and laughed at them hollowing and running back out and putting on their clothes.

We carried a wet bunch back to the park and let them out. As I recall, I never heard the words skinny dipping again. I think the icy water of the creek did it all the first time.

I always wondered how the girls got by, going in with wet clothes. Mama and Daddy were always at home and waiting on them when they came home. They had put the dry clothes on over a wet body. When we let them out at the park they all left running for home. I laughed at this for quite a while afterward.

The days of the old swim hole are gone. I would be afraid to go in a creek nowadays. The water was clean back then; nowadays there is no telling what is poured into the water. There used to be a spring with a bench, going up to Taylor Ridge. It no longer exists. We used to go skating at Pennsville and we would stop there and get a cold drink of water. Those day do not exist anymore, except in the memory of an old geezer.

Lonie Adcock of Rome is a retired Rome Police Department lieutenant. His latest book is "More Memories of the Old Geezer."

GUEST COLUMN: The bully of the town

Posted: Wednesday, February 17, 2016 6:00 am

The Bully of the Town was the name that my mother gave to this old folks' tale. This is one story that was told to us as kids. I have always doubted the story as being true. I have never tried to prove or disprove it. I believe that they told their kids this story to try to keep them on the straight and narrow.

This happened to a few people living in a community. It had a general store, a corn mill and, most of the time, a blacksmith shop. In other words, where the men would gather and play checkers and swap their bull stories. The cracker barrel was put out with the checkerboard every Saturday morning. This sounded great to see people together having fun and enjoying themselves. There was only one thing wrong, and I am going to tell it to you the way it was told to me as a kid.

Lonie Adcock

Lonie Adcock of Rome is a retired Rome Police Department lieutenant. His latest book, "More Memories of the Old Geezer," is now available.

There was a young man in the community by the name of Waldo. Waldo was what the old folks called a hell-raiser. Every Saturday night he would go to the Cross Road Saloon. Before the night was over, Waldo had started a fight with someone and beat him up. Waldo was one of them kind of people that seem to enjoy fighting. People that knew him stayed away from him. Waldo had no friends.

Tales were told of people who had been disfigured by Waldo. One such person was a young man Waldo started a fight with at the community general store. The story was that Waldo disfigured his face so badly that he left the community and never came back.

The worst one of the stories of Waldo was when he turned the preacher's buggy over with him and his family in it. It seemed that one Sunday morning after a night of fighting and carrying on, Waldo walked into the community church and began bullying the people. The Reverend tried to talk Waldo out of the church but to no avail. They watched as he scattered books and papers all over the church floor. The preacher was much of a man himself. He grabbed Waldo by the neck and the seat of the pants and shoved him out the door. Everyone thought Waldo was gone. He sat down on a bench and waited until church was over.

Church over with, the people headed for home. All the people were gone except a few who were standing around talking, when the preacher came out with his family. They got into their buggy — then Waldo ran out and grabbed the buggy. Waldo began to lift the side of the buggy from the ground. The preacher and his family fell from the buggy. Waldo then turned the buggy over on the side. He whipped the horse. The horse ran down the road, tearing the buggy to pieces. A bruised preacher and his family were carried home by a friend. The word went out over the community and Waldo strutted in front of the people.

The people in the community were God-fearing people and did not go out of the way looking for trouble. Waldo had most of the men afraid of him. Almost all of them. He was going to find out that there was one in the community that had no fear of Waldo the Bully.

I can not recall the name of the miller. He had a small grist mill that ground corn and other grain. Everyone called him The Miller. I will refer to him as The Miller in the rest of my story. The Miller was a small man by build, he was about 5 foot, 5 inches tall, around 130 pounds. It was said that lifting heavy bags of grain had given him strength that was unbelievable. He was much of a man, regardless of size.

The Miller stepped off his wagon and went into the general store. Waldo was across the street and saw him. He thought he would have some fun and let the people see how tough he was. He stood by the door and waited for The Miller to come out. The Miller had got his mail from the post office and was reading it as he came out onto the porch of the general store. Waldo struck his foot out in front o him and tripped him. He fell down the steps and into the dirt.

Then Waldo reached down, picking up The Miller with one hand. He threw him down into the dirt road and let out a laugh. But as he threw back his head to laugh aloud, yells of pain came from him. The Miller had picked up a piece of broken broom handle as he fell to the ground. With the broom handle he swung, hitting Waldo in the pit of his stomach. The second lick hit Waldo in the groin. Waldo hit the ground, screaming in pain.

The Miller jumped on his back, grabbing Waldo's coat and tying it around his head. He took the sleeves and tied them around Waldo's neck. His coat looked like a saddle. The Miller jumped on Waldo's back and began to ride him like a horse. The broom handle was used to whip him along. He would swing the stick and then bend over and whisper something in his ear. Around the general store yard, and then in to the store, Waldo went on all fours with The Miller on his back.

Finally Waldo came to a stop and fell to the ground, unable to move. The Miller bent over and again whispered into Waldo's ear. He stepped from Waldo's back and, picking up his mail, got into his wagon and left. The people stood in awe.

They watched as Waldo slowly got up to his feet. Removing his shirt from his head, he looked around. Not seeing The Miller he ran and got on his horse. As the story goes, Waldo was never again seen or heard about in the community. Being rode like a horse by a man half his size was too much to take.

Free from bullies, the community became the kind of place you enjoyed living in — it became a community of good, God-fearing people that you wanted as a neighbor.

Is this story true? I don't know. Did a man as small as The Miller ride a man as big as Waldo like a horse? I am not sure where this was supposed to have taken place. Maybe someday while researching a subject, you will run across where a man was rode like a horse while trying to be a big bad bully. Or just maybe this story was told to the young ones to keep them from becoming bullies. Either way, this is how I heard it from the old folks when I was a very small boy. No one ever knew what The Miller was whispering into Waldo's ear.

Lonie Adcock of Rome is a retired Rome Police Department lieutenant. His latest book is "More Memories of the Old Geezer."

GUEST COLUMN: The Spirit of friendship

Posted: Wednesday, March 2, 2016 6:00 am

Stories that were told by the old folks were supposed to be true. I have no way of proving or disproving this. I have always believed that it could have happened, but every time a story is handed down, things in the story will change. I will tell this one the way it was told to me as a kid.

It had been a bad year for farming. It rained in the spring and made planting late. When the plants began to grow it got hot and dry. Everything in the garden suffered from the heat and lack of rain. The corn got the size that was called nubbins. All the peas and other things that they used for swapping shriveled and withered away. They had nothing to trade with.

The man of the house gathered what he could and carried it to town. It left them wondering what tomorrow would bring.

The family had sat down for supper when they heard a knock on the front door. The man of the house went to see who was there. Standing in the yard was a man

Lonie Adcock

Lonie Adcock of Rome is a retired Rome Police Department lieutenant. His latest book, "More Memories of the Old Geezer," is now available.

dressed in buckskin. He wore moccasins and had a headband tied around his hair. He wore a black hat that resembled a top hat. He was Native American, there was no doubt.

When he spoke, it was perfect English. It was said that he sounded like a professor from an English college. He had a bedroll and stood still when he spoke. I remember my mother saying he didn't sound like the people they were used to talking to.

"Sir" he said, "my name is Ross, Stanley Ross. I am a teacher at a college in Oklahoma." He stuck out his hand and my great-grandfather shook hands with him. "May I lay my roll down?" he asked. My great-grandfather told him he could.

As the story went, he was born where the river made a bend just behind the house that they lived in. He wanted to camp out for a week where the village had been. He said that it was for spiritual reasons. Great Grandfather told him he could, and as he bent to pick up his roll, great-grandfather asked him if he would share their supper. He accepted and went out back to wash up. He was introduced to the family and showed a seat at the table. After supper he picked up his roll and headed out.

When the family all gathered in the living room, the man who said his name was Stanley Ross was the subject they talked about. No one knew who he really was or where he came from. One of the girls asked if anyone had noticed the ring he wore on his left hand. Then the ring became the subject they talked about. Bedtime came.

Early the next morning, Great Grandfather gathered some items that he thought he could trade and headed for town.

Great Grandmother went about doing her daily chores. A knock came at the door and she went to find the man who called himself Ross. He held a piece of pottery out to Great Grandmother, saying that he had dug it up and would like to give it to her. She thanked him for the vase and cleaned it up. It was an old piece and she put it in the center of the table.

Great Grandfather came back from town carrying a bag of groceries. Great Grandmother set in to fixing supper. Once supper was ready, Great Grandfather told her he was going to invite Ross up for supper. He headed to where Ross was camped. Ross met him with a smile. He again stuck out his hand and Great Grandfather invited him to the house for supper. He looked surprised that someone who had no more than Great Grandfather had was willing to share it with a stranger, but accepted.

At supper Ross began to talk in a low tone of voice. Everyone grew quiet and listened to his story.

They had moved him and his family from the village out to Oklahoma when he was a small boy. He had gone to school and become a teacher. His father had told him that a religious artifact was hidden where the village once stood. He had promised his father he would find it and bring it back to the tribe. He stated that, so far, he had no luck in finding it.

It was told that when Great Grandfather had moved them to the house on the river, one of the kids had found an artifact that looked like a cross with an Indian in full headdress on his knee praying. Above his head was what appeared to be a mist. It had been put in a paper wrap and covered with cloth to keep it from tarnishing, then put in a dresser drawer.

Great Grandfather shook his head, looking at Great Grandmother. She got up, went into the other room and came back with the cloth-wrapped artifact. She placed it in front of Ross and said, "Many times we had talked about trading this off for food. We would look at it and then put it back into the dresser drawer."

Ross looked up toward the ceiling and said something in the Cherokee language. He very gently unwrapped it. As he removed the paper from the artifact, everyone who was at the table will tell you that a glow came from it. Ross picked up the artifact and held it above his head and again spoke in the Cherokee language. He then gently wrapped it back up and put it in the center of the table.

He spoke, asking "What must I do to purchase this from you?" Great Grandfather picked up the artifact, looked at it and offered it to Ross. He took it in his hand, saying "You are good people and shall be rewarded." My great-grandfather replied, "No reward is necessary. It belonged to your people, take it with my blessing."

As Ross was leaving, he paused at the door. He again raised the artifact above his head and said something in Cherokee. He smiled and said, "I have asked the Great Spirit to bless this house and the people in it." Then he turned and went through the door.

The next day was Sunday and the family got ready for church. Great Grandfather went to where Ross was camped to invite him, but the camp site was cleaned up and looked as if no one had ever been there. As Great Grandfather stepped back up on the porch, he saw another vase like the one Ross had given them. He carried it into the house.

He put it on the table and reached inside to see what was wrapped inside of it. He pulled out a sheet of paper that Ross had written on. As he opened it, four coins fell onto the table. They all stood wide-eyed as Great Grandfather lined them up in a row. Four $20 gold coins. That was more money than they had ever seen at one time.

Great Grandfather picked up the paper and began to read. It went something like this: "Sir, in my travels from Oklahoma no one offered me any food or help. Your family is one in a million. I have recovered our medal that was worn by all who were chiefs of our tribe, thanks to you. I also recovered the tribe treasure and leave you and your family enough to get you through to your next planting." It was signed "Ross."

That story was told down though the years with this at the end — Do unto others as you would have others do unto you.

Lonie Adcock of Rome is a retired Rome Police Department lieutenant. His latest book is "More Memories of the Old Geezer."

GUEST COLUMN: Queasy feelings and gut instinct on the police force

Posted: Wednesday, March 16, 2016 6:15 am

It was one of those Saturday nights that a policeman doesn't look forward to. It had started when we came on at 11 p.m. and still going at 3 a.m. We managed to grab a few hamburgers and were headed back to East Rome when the dispatcher called us.

I picked up the mike, and he told us that someone had called in on a naked screaming woman.

He said there was some kind of disturbance at Buddy's Cafe on 12th Street. There was a convenience store next to Buddy's and in between them was a group of telephone booths. These telephones were how most of the people who lived in the project made calls. It was nothing unusual to come by there at all hours of the night and find two or three people on the telephone.

We pulled into that area and got out to look around. There on the concrete were pieces of clothing. A dress was torn in shreds; next to it was a blouse in the same condition. A big red woman's purse was on the

Lonie Adcock

Lonie Adcock of Rome is a retired Rome Police Department lieutenant. His latest book, "More Memories of the Old Geezer," is now available.

concrete with the pieces of clothes. Pete picked it up and looked inside. It was empty. He threw the purse on the back seat of the patrol car.

We headed down Crane Street and had got to the corner of 13th Street when I heard a whistle.

Pete pulled over and I got out. There on the porch of the house stood a man. He came out to meet us. "Officer," he said. "I don't expect you to believe me, but I just saw a woman run by naked and screaming. What you are not going to believe is she had a snake wrapped around her neck."

He kept on talking. "I was standing on the porch smoking me a cigarette when she came around the corner of the house into the yard. I got a good look at her. She was naked except for a bra and a snake wrapped around her head." He pointed to the end of the street where a light shined though an open door. He turned, and saying "that's all I got to say," he opened the door and went inside.

"You heard what the man said. Let's go down to where the light is shining though the open door," I said. Pete pulled from the curb and started down the street to the house with the light and open door. I remember to this day what Pete said getting out of the car. "I hope she has got on some clothes and got rid of her snake necklace."

Walking up to the door, I could see someone inside sitting on a couch. I knocked on the door; she opened the screen and stepped out on the porch. We asked her if she was all right and if that was her running naked though the street screaming. We were assured that it was not her and everything was all right, so we got back into the car and left. Pete pulled back out to Buddy's place on 12th Street. There we talked for a few minutes. Back on patrol, the night went fast.

We came to the conclusion that someone had put a purse with a snake in it in the telephone booth. When she saw it she covered the purse from view, but when she opened the purse the snake went down the front of her blouse. She then went into tearing off her clothes. With everything except her bra torn off, the snake wrapped around her neck. I have no idea where the snake fell off.

I bet that it was a sight to see. A 200 pound woman wearing a bra and a snake around her neck, running down the street screaming.

Other days on the police force brought out a different kind of queasy feeling.

This was when a certain kind of call would come to me and I would get out of the car, stand still and listen for a few minutes before sticking my head into a hornet's nest.

When I was growing up I had that feeling in my stomach. Those that had it called it a gut instinct. If something was going to happen that wasn't right, the gut feeling would hit you.

I remember one time when my partner threw all caution to the wind and rushed up to the front door where we had got a call. That queasy feeling told me something wasn't right.

The door came open and a gun was stuck into my partner's stomach. I had gotten beside the door, out of sight. The man let out a few choice words, telling the officer what he was going to do. Then he stuck his head out of the door, looking for me. I placed my gun against his head and, in a few choice words, told him what I was going to do if he didn't hand me his gun. He hesitated then handed me the gun. We carried him to jail and booked him. The queasy feeling had paid off.

Another time I found the door to the Pontiac place torn open. We surrounded the building and began a search. We went from one end of the building to the other, but nothing was out of place. I was standing in the middle of the auto shop when that queasy feeling hit me.

I called the officers over and told them to do another search. I was standing under a beam that ran across the building that was used to hook a block and tackle. They would pull motors and other heavy parts from the automobiles. The officers came back shaking their heads; nothing was found. Then a cold chill went down my back and I looked up at the beam. I could see a shoe sticking out. With the beam covered by the officers, I found the lights and turned them on. When the lights came on he sat up to where we could see him. The queasy feeling had paid off again.

I remember another time my partner and I had a warrant for a subject. We had gone through the house and looked everywhere we thought a man could hide. I had not been in the kitchen; my partner had searched it. He shook his head saying, "I had it from a good source that he is here in this house." I walked over to the kitchen sink, and that old queasy feeling hit me in the stomach.

I turned, looking at everything in the kitchen. Over in the corner was a small closet. I went over and opened the door. My partner came over saying, "I have looked in there several times." But I noticed that the closet didn't have the space in it that it should have. I took my hand and pushed up on the boards that were over head. One of then fell out and a foot came through. I grabbed it and yanked. He came down with a few cans of stuff with him. He let out a yell as he hit the floor. We gathered him up and carried him to the jail and booked him. The queasy feeling paid off.

I guess a lot of people have what they call the old gut feeling. Some choose to ignore it, others will pay attention to it. What it is, I don't know. But I would say that if you have a queasy feeling that ties a knot in your stomach, turn around and get the heck out of there.

Lonie Adcock of Rome is a retired Rome Police Department lieutenant. He will be signing his new book, "Fact or Fiction" from 3 to 5 p.m. Thursday at the Last Stop Gift Shop by the Rome Civic Center.

on Jackson Hill.

GUEST COLUMN: Homer the ax-toting ghost

Posted: Wednesday, March 30, 2016 6:15 am

I can remember a lot of stories the old folks told to us kids as we were growing up. Storytelling was like going to the movies on a Saturday night. Some of the old folks could come up with good ghost stories. As I have said, I could not prove that any of them were true. True or false, they made good listening.

Supper over and the kitchen cleaned up, my mother would come out and get in her favorite chair to relax. We would all gather around her and she knew what we were waiting for. She would sit silent for a few minutes, then she would ask, "Have you heard the one of Homer the ax-toting ghost?" We hadn't heard of Homer, so she would tell it to us.

It went this way:

Homer was a woodcutter who lived in the neighborhood. He sawed down trees and split them into firewood. Most of the people in the neighborhood bought their firewood from Homer.

Lonie Adcock

Lonie Adcock of Rome is a retired Rome Police Department lieutenant. His latest book, "More Memories of the Old Geezer," is now available.

To hear my mother describe him was something else. Homer stood 6 foot 6 inches tall, without an ounce of fat on him. He was single and most of the young girls that lived in the area would let out a sigh when he went by.

All the people that knew Homer knew he was in love with Sadie Mae Hopkins, who lived in the big house on the hill. Sadie Mae was known by all to be the most beautiful girl around. Homer and Sadie had to slip around to be together. Her father, Burrell Hopkins, had swore to kill any man he caught with Sadie. But young love has no boundaries, so Homer and Sadie had a meeting place — and every chance they got, they would meet.

Homer kept the woodpile high, and in the winter it was known that he made good money. He was well-liked by all the people and would boast that he had a lot of money saved up. Was money the cause of the fate that fell upon Homer? No one ever knew. He was around one day with his wood, and the next day he was gone.

The people in the area would go by to order wood, but Homer could not be found. It was reported to the sheriff and an investigation was made. For several months they searched, but could not find him.

Homer had been missing for about a month when Burrell Hopkins reported that Sadie Mae was missing. The people in the community just assumed that she and Homer had run away together. It was known how they felt about each other. Time passed — weeks turned into months and months into years — but no Homer and Sadie Mae were ever found.

Time ran out and Homer's house was sold at a county auction for taxes. The once-fine house now needed repairs. A couple bought the house and restored it back to what it looked like when Homer lived in it. They moved into the house one week. And back out a few days later.

They told the people in the community the house was haunted. It stood vacant and was again sold for taxes. The house was rented and my great-grandfather and great-grandmother moved into it.

Grandmother was pleased with the house and bragged about it. But things aren't always what they seem to be.

One night, a noise in the kitchen brought grandmother from her bed. She walked into the kitchen to find a man with an ax in his hand standing there. She stopped in her tracks and said nothing. The man slowly turned and looked straight at grandmother. Then he raised his ax and ran at her. He passed though her and went out the back door.

Grandmother was a small woman but, as Grandfather would say, "Susan was not afraid of old Billy Hell himself." She stood her ground and watched as the figure went through the door and outside. She ran to the door and opened it. She looked around outside. It was a bright moonlit night, but she could see nothing.

After several more incidents, she told Grandfather what had begun to happen.

There began a vigil in the kitchen. They would take time about sitting up to catch the man with the ax. Grandmother would tell their family, "They can't hurt you if you don't let them."

The way the story goes, they were sitting and drinking a coffee after the rest of the family had gone to bed. The man with the ax came through the door. They kept on drinking their coffee. He gestured with the ax for them to follow him. They followed him outside. He went to a small rise at the back of the house and began to dig with the ax. They watched as he said one word: "There." Then he disappeared and they went back into the house.

At breakfast the next morning it was decided they would try to get the sheriff out to dig in the spot that Homer's ghost had showed them.

Rather hesitantly, the sheriff brought a trustee with a shovel from the jail. He thought he was on a wild goose chase. The trustee sank the shovel into the soft dirt. A few shovels full and human bones began to appear. It was determined that there were two bodies buried in the shallow grave.

The sheriff took the bones back to the jail and examined a ring they found with them. The skeleton remains turned out to be of Homer and Sadie.

With pressure put on Burrell Hopkins, he confessed that he had shot at Homer and Sadie jumped between them. Sadie fell to the ground with a load of buckshot in her. He then turned the gun on Homer. They fell side by side. Burrell had dug a shallow grave and buried them both beside a big oak tree. He lived with the fact that he had killed his only daughter.

The story goes that people came from far and wide and dug for Homer's money. It was never found. My mother would tell how you could look up the hill to where the bodies were buried and see them on a moonlit night. They would stand at the oak tree embraced as lovers would. Burrell died in prison for the murder of Homer and Sadie Mae.

Lonie Adcock of Rome is a retired Rome Police Department lieutenant. His latest book is "Fact or Fiction."

GUEST COLUMN: The house on the hill

Posted: Wednesday, April 13, 2016 6:00 am

It sat on a small hill at the rear of the community. Most folks knew that it was the home of the Schultzes. In its heyday it had been a mansion as big and as good as any in the world. Old man Henie Schultz built it when he migrated from Germany to the States. It was known that he had come when an overthrow of power in Germany took place.

The story goes that Henie was an overbearing person. He got pleasure in other people's suffering. He bought up land and became one of the richest people in the county. He would lend money and go to court and take their land if they couldn't pay.

He lived high in the neighborhood until one day a deliveryman found Henie and his wife dead in the kitchen. It was murder, but no one was ever caught and made to pay for it. It was rumored that law enforcement officers never tried to catch the guilty one, because the people were glad that he was gone.

Lonie Adcock

Lonie Adcock of Rome is a retired Rome Police Department lieutenant. His latest book, "More Memories of the Old Geezer," is now available.

The house stayed empty and the county took it for taxes. They held a sale, but no one would buy it. The people in the community would tell you that the house was haunted by Henie and his wife. It was said that Henie's wife had a garden that grew vegetables that no one could compete with. Although the house wasn't lived in, the garden grew back every year. The people would not bother the vegetables in the garden and called them ghost food.

Then Benny came along.

A family by the name of Garrett moved into the community and had a boy by the name of Benny. People began to miss items around their homes. Some found their houses had been broken into and ransacked. The neighborhood was in an uproar and a deputy was sent from the sheriff's office. The name of the deputy has stayed with me down though the years. His name was Rufus — a 6-footer who was strictly business. He didn't play games with those who broke the law.

Rufus went though the community talking to the people. He came to the house where Benny lived.

With the family gathered around, he made it plain he was going to catch the guilty one and put him in jail. While he was talking he noticed a smirk on Benny's face and knew he had hit home. He knew it would only be a matter of time before he would catch Benny in the act.

It was a bright moonlit night when Deputy Rufus got on his horse and began to patrol. He sat in the shadow of a big oak tree and watched the store and grist mill. He had stepped down to stretch when he heard the breaking of glass. He tied up his horse and moved toward the store. He found a window with the glass broken, raised it and eased inside.

Pulling his gun from his holster, he moved quietly through the store.

Sitting in a chair, eating a cake, was Benny. A cigar lay on the edge of the counter with smoke curling upward from it. Benny reached over and took a puff and put it back on the counter. The smoke hardly out of his mouth, he took a bite of the cake. He was having himself a good time and didn't hear Deputy Rufus until he stopped beside him.

Benny turned and jumped to his feet, striking Deputy Rufus and knocking him backward. The deputy hit his head as he went down, knocking himself unconscious. Benny ran, jumping out the window and heading for the woods. He ran until he could run no more. He sat down to get his breath.

There in front of him was the Henie Schultz house. This, he thought, would be a good place to hide, for no one ever came to the house.

Benny found a broken window with a board nailed over it. He pulled on the board and it came loose. He crawled in. He could see that he had entered a big foyer. He looked through an open door and saw what appeared to be a big ballroom. The ceiling let off an eerie light. There were stars and the moon painted on the ceiling. A cold chill went though him and he was thrown to the floor.

Later, he told the deputy the Devil came and picked him up, and he began to cry. The Devil shook him and told him to shut up. He was taken into another room that had a table and there sat a man and woman. He had heard of Henie and his wife and knew that this was who he was looking at. He was forced into a chair and the man began to talk. The Devil stood by with a smile on his face.

He was told that he would have to go out into the garden and pick some vegetables. Benny said he knew that if he got the chance he was going to get away from there as fast as possible.

The story went that he was given a basket and led to the door by the Devil. He walked out into the garden alone. He looked back to see the man and woman standing in the door with the Devil. He then threw down the basket and began to run toward the village. He ran as far as he could and fell down in the road. He said he passed out.

The deputy found Benny in the road and carried him back to the community store. There, with some of the community leaders, he listened to Benny's story. No one spoke as Benny described the man and woman and they knew he was right. They also knew that Benny had never seen them when they were alive. As for the Devil, they only shook their heads. Benny was carried to the city where he served time for burglary. The one thing that amazed everyone there was how a 16-year-old boy could have solid gray hair.

You would think that this would be the end of the story. There was more to come.

Benny came back home and got a job and settled down. He would never talk about the house on the hill to anyone. The house stood out on the hill and most people would look the other way when passing it. All was quiet until one night the people were awakened by a red glow coming from the hill. The house was on fire. They gathered to watch; no one tried to put it out.

The house burned down with nothing but two chimneys left standing. Soon after, Benny left the community, never to be seen again. Everyone felt that Benny had burned the house down.

Is this a true story or was it made up by the old folks to try to keep their kids from dong wrong? Maybe it was just a story, but on moonlit nights the people would gather to watch Henie and his wife work in the vegetable garden. And standing on the side was a figure that looked like the creature Benny had described.

Lonie Adcock of Rome is a retired Rome Police Department lieutenant. His latest book is "Fact or Fiction."

GUEST COLUMN: Oh, it's Saturday night

Posted: Wednesday, April 27, 2016 6:00 am

Did you ever wonder what young teenagers did for fun back in the old days?

There were a few who could afford a car to ride around in on a Saturday night. Most of the poor boys had to find another way. There were parties at someone's house. Most of the mothers didn't have time to supervise a party so the poor boys didn't have them.

If you were lucky and had a car and the money for the price of a ticket, there was the drive-in. It didn't take a lot of money to go to the drive-in. I was working but had other obligations, so money was scarce with me. I had a friend who had a car, but when we had a short payday week the car had to sit.

When we had the money, there were skating rinks around. There were none in Rome at that time. Some of the old folks thought a couple on the floor skating was playing into the hands of the Devil. Rollerskating was looked upon as dancing — an instrument to lure

Lonie Adcock

Lonie Adcock of Rome is a retired Rome Police Department lieutenant. His latest book, "More Memories of the Old Geezer," is now available.

the young people into a devil's life. I skated just about anywhere there was a skating rink. I can't recall ever meeting the Devil on a pair of skates, but I met a lot of people who were, as the old saying goes, "as mean as the Devil."

Some of boys found a spring back in the woods off of Horseleg Creek Road. We went down one Saturday and cleaned out the area to where we could get our cars in. We didn't, at that time, realize the small building that we passed going to the spring was the city's powder house. It was where all the dynamite and other blasting powder was kept.

We cleared an area around the spring and pulled in some logs to sit on. It was a beautiful spring and the area was full of dogwood trees in bloom. We thought that we had found us a place to come to on Saturday nights.

The word was passed among our group and as darkness fell we began to gather. A small fire was built and the wieners were placed on the sticks and held over the fire. The mustard and ketchup was placed on a tree stump and the fun began.

We were eating and singing and having a good old time when someone came up behind me and put his hand on my shoulder. I looked up and, standing there, was the biggest man I have ever seen. He had a gun on his hip. He shook his head, motioning for me to be quiet. He sat down, but there was another one standing. He whispered in my ear and I will never forget what he said. "If you don't want to go to jail you will be quiet."

I had no hankering to go to jail so I sat as quiet as a mouse. He again whispered in my ear. "Put a wiener on a stick and hand it to me." I put a wiener on a stick and handed it to him. No one else had seen the men, for they were busy having a good time. He placed the wiener over the fire and I watched him. He checked it and I handed him a bun. With mustard and ketchup on it, he began to eat. The other one had moved around to where he could see the ones on the other side of the fire.

Then the one who was standing up spoke. I will remember what he said as long as I live. "Boys and girls just sit tight and enjoy yourselves. There is no reason to be afraid of us; we just came by to have a hot dog with you." He took a stick from the stump and placed a wiener on it. He then sat down and fixed himself a hot dog.

Carlton had started to tell a ghost story but had stopped. The man sitting beside me told him go ahead, that he would love to hear the story. I must say Carlton outdid himself that night in the telling of the story. They stayed a while and ate several more hot dogs. They left, telling us that everything was OK.

They returned several more times and enjoyed the hot dogs and we had a lot of fun at the spring — until one night we went down and someone had put a cable across the road.

We had tried to stay in the park after dark but a man who lived across the street from the park would call the police. They came out and put up signs stating that no one was to be in the park after 8 o'clock. The people who lived around the park called the old man, who called the police to us. The old grouch box.

I cleaned off a spot in my garden and decided to have a marshmallow roast in the back yard. We had the usual crowd and the roast started. We kept the noise down and no one bothered us. I had gone into the house when one of the girls came up for a drink of water. I got the marshmallows and went back to the fire. I don't recall who the girl was, but she came back to the fire laughing.

Someone asked what was so funny. She then told them about this big clothespin that my mother had on a table. She would put bills in it when they came in. She said that she had asked my mother what she used the clothespin for, and my mother had said it was what held up my diaper when I was a small child.

Lonie Adcock of Rome is a retired Rome Police Department lieutenant. His latest book is "Fact or Fiction."

GUEST COLUMN: Some people I have known

Posted: Wednesday, May 18, 2016 6:15 am

I remember back when I was growing up that there always seemed to be an old drunk in the neighborhood. The ones that I am writing about were some of those I met while on the Police Department. I know that they were human beings and most of them had a good heart in them. The reason that someone becomes an old drunk is beyond my knowledge.

Back when I went on the Police Department there were five police officers on Broad Street and two cars. The Cotton Block was the beat that ran from the South Rome Bridge to the middle of the second block on Broad.

At that time, there were five beer joints on the Cotton Block. There was someone in them most of the time. On Saturday night it was booming. One officer had the beat. You worked the traffic until it slowed down, then you went into the beer joints trying to keep them quiet.

Lonie Adcock

Lonie Adcock of Rome is a retired Rome Police Department lieutenant. His latest book is "Fact or Fiction."

Back in my young day I done some hanging out at the Maple Street Gymnasium. I got to know a well-known boxer of this area. I will call him Carl. I do not mention last names, for I do not intend to cause anyone embarrassment.

Carl would teach boys how to box and the art of good sportsmanship. All the boys liked him. Carl went out and made a name for himself as a boxer. I lost track of him for quite a few years. In 1958 I went on the City of Rome Police Department and again came in contact with Carl.

I walked into the Bumble Bee Cafe one Saturday night. There was one man sitting at the counter, drinking a beer. I stopped at the back and talked to the lady who ran the cafe. She pointed to the man at the counter and said, "Watch that fellow." I took a good look at the man and my heart began to pound. I could not believe my eyes. There, sitting and drinking a beer was my old boxing teacher Carl.

I walked back to where he sat and stopped. He sensed my presence and turned on the stool to face me. He stared at me and then, to my surprise, he smiled and said, "I don't believe it." He struck out his hand and I took it. I waited to see if he could call my name. He said, "Adcock, where have you been? I haven't seen you in years." I remember making a remark that I had been here and there. We talked for a while and then I hit the street, making my rounds.

I learned that Carl had made it to the big time but alcohol had brought him down. He told me that he was going to quit drinking anything and get himself a job. Every time I talked to him I would remind him of what he had said. True to his word, he quit drinking and got a job at Trends Mill. He drove a truck for them. He turned his life around and, as I told him, made an old Maple Street Gym boy proud of him.

When I went on the Police Department, if you worked the street and needed a car you had to call on the pay telephone. The nickel you put into the telephone came out of the officer's pocket. No matter how many calls you made, the money was never given back to you. Now a nickel don't sound like much nowadays, but take a week where you had to call a car 10 or 15 times and you can see where you came up a Krystal burger short at eating time.

I was checking out the parking lot behind the Bumble Bee Cafe when I found a man lying in the alleyway. I managed to get him to the front of the cafe and sat him down on the sidewalk. He was mumbling and was in a drunk stupor. I took everything out of my pocket, searching for a nickel. I didn't have one.

I remember saying out loud, "Of all things, I don't have a nickel." I felt a tug on my pants leg and looked down. The old drunk was stretching out his hand to me. I started to say something when I noticed that he was holding a nickel between his fingers. I reached down and took it, saying, "Thank you." In a slurred voice, he said, "You are welcome."

The Cotton Block was known to be a rough beat. It was known among the police officers as the Hell Hole.

This story started like so many Saturday nights before. First the street, then the beer joints. It had just got dark and I began to make my rounds when a noise behind the Spur Gas Station drew my attention. I went up on the railroad's tracks and looked toward the trestle. Hearing but not seeing any thing, I moved down the tracks.

As I got close to the wholesale house, it grew quiet. I walked into the street that ran in front of the wholesale house. As I approached, someone ran from behind, grabbing me, taking me to the ground. I know now that whoever had a hold of me was a very strong person. I remembered afterward that his breath was on the back of my neck. I also remember that there was not the smell of alcohol on his breath.

Whoever had a hold of me had lured me into the dark so he could attack me. I was doing everything I could to get loose when I heard a thump. The hold was released and the subject fell to the ground. I turned to face who had hit him. Old Charlie, a homeless man who lived under the bridge, stood looking at me with a board in his hand. "Officer Adcock," he said. "Are you all right?" I picked up my cap saying, "Here, go and call me a car." "I have already called you a car," he said.

I heard the patrol car as it crossed the bridge. They turned into the street where I was and came to a stop. I motioned for them to get the one lying in the street. As they pulled off with the man who had attacked me, I turned to Charlie. He told me that he had watched the man come into the back street and start to make noise. When he saw me he knew what was happening. He went and called for a car and then came back to help me.

I was assigned to a patrol car and lost sight of him, but I will always be in debt to an old drunk whom they called Charlie.

I have known a lot of what people call old drunks in my life. Some are mean, but most of them become addicted to alcohol. Many a good man has been brought down and sent to their grave by alcohol. The one who gave me the nickel to call the car was found on the riverbank dead. Carl put his life back on track and made me proud of him.

I always remember that old drunks are human beings who have got off track and need help to get back.

Lonie Adcock of Rome is a retired Rome Police Department lieutenant. His latest book is "Fact or Fiction."

GUEST COLUMN: Days of white lightning and mountain dew

Posted: Wednesday, June 1, 2016 6:00 am

Down South when you talk of white lightning, everyone knows what you are talking about. Back in the old days most of the people made their own. Some made it and delivered it to the city to be sold.

White whiskey, made right, was drunk by grown-up males and some females. Other names I remember are moonshine, booze, white lightning, firewater, rot gut and mountain dew. I am sure there are other names for it.

I remember my first chase of a bootlegger's car when I went on the police department. It was one of those quiet nights, and so the old veteran police officer let the rookie drive the car. We were on Maple Street when we passed a car running with his lights off. I turned and started after the car.

When he saw the police car, he let the hammer down. We went down Fourteenth Street to Flannery, then onto a short street that led to the old Cole Stadium. We

Lonie Adcock

Lonie Adcock of Rome is a retired Rome Police Department lieutenant. His latest book is "Fact or Fiction."

went back onto Flannery and onto Fourteenth and then around a house that was occupied by a lady named Mabel. We were on his bumper, pushing his car, so we went around and around until he managed to straighten out and go down Fourteenth Street. I made an extra run around the house before I could follow, but he had gone out of sight.

I stopped on Flannery and turned off the lights and siren. Then, from down Flannery Street, we heard a loud crash. We knew that he had wrecked. I eased down the street with the light off until we saw the car in a ditch. He was trying to get it out but the ditch was too deep. When we pulled up, he cut the motor, crawled out and came over to where we were in the road. He was laughing. He had enjoyed the chase but, this being my first, it was kind of annoying to me. We carried him to headquarters and booked him in. We found several gallons of white whiskey in the car.

I never had the desire to go though someone's house searching for moonshine whiskey, but the local revenue agent had a habit of calling for me and my partner to help him if he was going to raid a house.

On this Sunday morning we got a call to Smith Street. The house was occupied by a lady by the name of Hattie. We checked out and met the revenue agent. I told them I would sit in the living room and watch the suspect while they searched the house. As I watched her, her face changed when one of the searchers got close to the window. It was pure panic if they touched the framing around the window. I knew where her whiskey was hidden.

The others were in the rest of the house. I went over to the window. I took a hold of the frame and gave it a jerk. The frame slid out and inside of the windowsill were several bottles of white whiskey. I called the others back and showed it to them.

The searchers decided that, having found the whiskey in the windowsill, they would go outside. I moved the owner of the house outside to the back yard. The search began again and I watched her face. No sign until someone came close to the woodpile. Pure panic showed as they moved a few sticks around on the stack of wood. Her face showed fear as one of the officer sat down on the chopping block; her face gave her away.

I got up and walked over to the chopping block. I called for the revenue agent. He came over shaking his head. "What's the matter?" I asked. "I don't think she has any more," he said. I pointed to the chopping block. "Move the block." I watched as he turned the block over. There, under the block, was a hole — and in the hole sat three gallon-cans of white whiskey. He turned to me and asked, "How did you know?" I laughed and said, "Psychic."

Of course, anyone who knows will tell you I am not psychic.

Another time, my partner and I were going down East First Street when we saw Hattie and another woman. Hattie was carrying a gallon glass container full of a white liquid. I noticed there was a bead around the top of the liquid. When I pulled over she held up the container and, laughing, asked "Would you like a drink?" I got out and walked around the car to her. I reached out and took the container and pure panic lit up her face. "I believe I will, Hattie," I said.

I put the container on the truck of the patrol car. "It's kerosene," she said in a small voice. I screwed the top off the container. The smell hit me before the top was loose. It was what most drinkers called rot gut whiskey. My partner got out of the car and put the cuffs on her. I reached out and felt of a pocket that was on a jacket she wore. I took out a 22-caliber nine-shot revolver. We booked her into the sheriff's jail.

The judge gave Hattie a year, with six months to serve and the rest on probation. I got out of the car and went back to walking a beat on Broad Street. No one was more surprised the day I found Hattie cooking in a restaurant on Broad. She had served her time and went to work and had got married.

Now, back in those days the Cotton Block was known to be a rough part of Broad. From after dark until closing time, there was always something going on.

It was getting close to closing time when a car pulled in front of the cafe where Hattie worked. They begin to shout and use foul language. I went over to see what was going on. I stepped up on the sidewalk from the road and was jumped by two subjects. I threw one against the car and he fell to the sidewalk. The other one caught me in a hold that I could not break.

Then, from nowhere, a loud crack like glass breaking and the smell of beer. He turned me loose and fell to his knees. I ran his arm though the bumper of the car. I then cuffed the two together. I heard someone behind me, turned and was surprised to see Hattie holding a broken bottle. I knew then that Hattie had saved the day for me.

With the two on the way to jail, I went into the cafe where Hattie and the owner were. I went into the restroom and cleaned up as much as I could. Then I went to Hattie. I told her how much I appreciated the help, but asked, "Why did you do it?"

I will always remember what she said. "I knew you needed help and I couldn't stand still and let them hurt my friend." I smiled, and she added, "You, being physic, already knew why I helped you." She was indeed a true friend for not many people I put in jail would help me. Down though the years, though, I had a few that did. That was a long time ago but I still remember them and they will always have a place in my heart.

Lonie Adcock of Rome is a retired Rome Police Department lieutenant. His latest book is "Fact or Fiction."

GUEST COLUMN: Raw Head and Bloody Bones

Posted: Wednesday, June 15, 2016 6:00 am

Back when I was growing up, parents knew where their kids were. If they told you to stay in the yard, you stayed in the yard.

That wasn't always the way it was, though. There has never, in my belief, been a kid that did everything their parents told them.

In my days, the hickory switch helped me to listen when my parents spoke. I walked the line most of the time, but on an occasion I strayed from the path. When I did and got caught, I got a dusting on the seat of my pants for it. That hurt my pride more than the seat of my pants.

Parents had other way of keeping their children close to home. One way was the telling of a creature that they called Raw Head.

Raw Head walked the dark streets at night looking for boys and girls who stayed out late at night. If you were doing an errand for your parents, Raw Head would know it and leave you alone. If you got out on your own, he also knew.

Lonie Adcock

Lonie Adcock of Rome is a retired Rome Police Department lieutenant. His latest book is "Fact or Fiction."

He would take a potion and rub it on your head and all the hair would come off. The head would stay raw for a while and the skin on the head would grow back slick. I remember looking at bald-headed men and smiling to myself. I knew that they had been bad, and old Raw Head had got a hold of them.

Old Bloody Bones was another creature that lurked in dark places.

If you walked by, he would try to get you into the dark where he was. If you went in, he would rub his bloody bones on you. You would have to run home and take a bath or you would look like old Bloody Bones.

There was a woman called Soap Sally, who walked around carrying a sack on her shoulder. Soap Sally would take mean boys and girls and make them into soap.

Now, Soap Sally lived in a house down by the tracks. I would take the long way around in order not to get too close to her. It was a known fact that she made soap and sold it to a small store that was on Allen Street. I wondered where she got all the mean boys and girls to make the soap. We never had anyone go missing in our neighborhood.

There was a creature that lived in the woods called Booger Bear. He was a big hairy animal that looked like an oversized bear.

Booger Bear roamed the woods looking for mean kids. He would catch them and take them to his cave. Once in the cave, you would be cleaned and cooked in a big pot of boiling water. I have often wondered if you were made into soup or stew. I can't recall anyone who came up missing from being in the woods.

There was the ax man, who walked the woods looking for boys who disobeyed their parents. He wore boots and overalls. His trademark was a solid red shirt. If he was ever described to you, you would know him on sight. The axe was a double-bladed one. It was big and shiny.

One day I sneaked off down to the creek early and found a place that the water had gone down and left it full of water. I saw fish swimming in the water, but it was not deep enough to cover them. I ran back home and got me some trot line and went back to get the fish.

I took off my shoes and socks and put them on the bank. I rolled up my pants legs and waded in to get the fish. He was a big one and gave me trouble getting him out onto the bank. I took the cord and ran it though his gill and tied it so I could carry it. I sat down on a log and put my shoes and socks on.

As I was getting up, I caught a movement out the corner of my eye. There, coming toward me, was a man wearing a red shirt and carrying an axe on his shoulder. That was the biggest shiny axe I had ever seen. I hit the trail out of the woods running. I left my fish, for I knew the man I saw was the axe man. I ran up on my front porch and fell into a swing.

I had ran so hard and fast that I felt like my heart was going to burst. I sat still so that my mother wouldn't see me. I had just got my breath back when my mother came to the door. She open it, saying, "Lonie, come with me." I followed her through the house to the back door. She stepped out onto the porch with me following her. I came to a sudden stop — for standing there was the axe man, with his axe on his shoulder and holding my fish.

I must have drawed back but he smiled and held out the fish. "I believe this is your fish," he said. I took the fish but stayed out of his reach. I wasn't going to let him hit me with that big shiny axe. I watched him as he left, knowing that I was in for it.

My mother took the fish and put him in a pail of water. "Now young man, you and I are going to have a long talk." I am here to tell you that the talk we had didn't hurt the ears but there was no dust left on the seat of my pants.

After all the years have passed, we know that there were no such creatures as Raw Head and Bloody Bones.

There was a lady in the neighborhood who carried a sack on her shoulder, but taking boys and turning them into soap? Impossible. A bear creature that made stew out of mean boys? No way.

I did find out that the axe man lived on Allen Street. He made willow chairs. They said that the seat looked like strips of bark peeled from the willow that he used to work with. I looked at the chair bottom and it looked like dried skin.

The other creatures I do not believe in, but the axe man? It's debatable.

Lonie Adcock of Rome is a retired Rome Police Department lieutenant. His latest book is "Fact or Fiction."

The Vaseline man of Rome

Posted: Wednesday, June 22, 2016 8:30 am

I went on the police department in June of 1958. I had to work third shift for a few months before rotating to the first shift. Coming off of nights and hitting the street in the daytime was quite an event.

Back then, everything focused on Broad Street. When the street wasn't bumper to bumper with traffic, it gave you a chance to meet and make new friends. I would go around to the stores and make friends with the people on the block. It wasn't too long before the people got to know me.

The Vaseline man of Rome

LONIE ADCOCKGUEST COLUMNIST

I had always been a people-watcher, and on a busy day Broad Street was full of people to watch.

One such person was a gentleman who ran a clothing store. He would come out in the morning and go get a paper. He would head down Broad to Enloe Drug Store for a cup of coffee. He always had a frown on his face and never smiled.

I would say "good morning" every time he crossed the street in front of me. I kept this up for several weeks, with him never answering me. Then to my surprise he passed me, took a few steps, turned and said "good morning." From then on, he seemed to try beating me to saying "good morning." I would stop and talk to him when he was standing in his store, not busy. He got to where he would buy an extra cup of coffee in the morning, one for me.

Another person who always caught my interest was a young man who rode a bicycle up Broad Street in the mornings. If it was cool, not cold, he wore a swimsuit. When the weather got cold he wore exercise outfits with what we called tennis shoes. They were red. On the hot days he wore the swimsuit with the red tennis shoes.

I had noticed that he always looked like his skin was greasy. On a hot day you could see where the grease on his body had run. A towel lay in the basket on the bicycle, and when he stopped for the red light he would rub himself down with the grease that was on his body. I would look at him and wonder what was with him and the greasy body.

He violated no law by wearing a swimsuit in public, so there was no reason to ask him. I watched him for quite a while, riding his bicycle and wearing his swim suit and red tennis shoes, not knowing that one day I would come head to head with him.

There was another young man in his 20s who was fascinating to watch. He walked with a crutch under one arm. At that time I was in my 30s and he could take that crutch and walk Broad Street twice to my once. He worked in a store on Broad and you could see him all though the day. It was amazing to see him get around.

I was at Second and Broad watching the traffic one day when my captain came up to me. Shift was set to change and when he started to talk I knew that I didn't like what he was saying. He was telling me that I was going to be assigned to a patrol car with a partner.

He didn't ask if I wanted to be in a car; he told me I was. He was the captain. But when he told me I would be riding with the Whizz, I felt better. I worked the street with the Whizz and knew him. He was one of the best.

The Whizz was a veteran police officer and I was a rookie. You would have never known it, though, for when making a decision the Whizz let you have your say.

Some of the older officers at that time treated a rookie as if he didn't know anything. They were the boss and you followed. Not the Whizz. You were half of the team and he let you know you were. I have often wondered what would have happened if I had been put with some of the others for, you see, I was never any good at following. I have always had a mind of my own.

It went well with the Whizz and we became a team. I had a lot of good riding partners while on the department but the Whizz was the best.

Then came one of those hot muggy nights when all the windows in the patrol car were down. We did not have air conditioning in the cars at that time. Rules were that the cap was to be worn at all times in the car. Rule broken. It was so hot that the caps were lying on the seat. It was one of those nights when you had sweat circles under the arms.

We had pulled in at Myrtle Hill and stepped outside of the car when dispatch called. I picked up the mike and told him to go ahead. He gave us a disturbance call on the lower end of Pennington Avenue. We got back in the car. I remember I was driving. When I pulled in to the front of the house, everything was quiet.

Whizz checked out and I turned off the motor and followed him up to the front of the house. We stood and listened but everything was still quiet. There was about six steps going up onto the porch. I started up with my hand on the rail. Whizz had just stepped up on the bottom step. Then, from out of the darkness, something or someone came at me at a high rate of speed.

Whatever it was, it hit me on the shoulder — turning me around on the steps. I grabbed for a railing and stopped my fall. I heard the Whizz let out a yell. I jumped to the ground and ran over to where Whizz lay. I dropped to my knees and rolled Whizz over on his back. He slowly sat up. Then he shook his head and said, "What in the hell was that?"

I stood up, looking around. I could not see anything in the street. I reached and helped Whizz to his feet. I walked back toward the house; someone had come out on the porch. A man stood at the top of the steps with a gun in his hand. I stopped and told the man to put the gun down, that we were the police. He handed the gun to a woman, saying "put this by the bed." He came down the steps to where I stood. The Whizz came over to us.

We talked for a few minutes then went up on the porch to look at a window. The screen was torn off and marks were on the window where someone had tried to pry it open. We started to leave, telling the man we would keep a check on his house. He informed us that if someone came through the window he had better have his insurance paid up.

We went back to the station, for I had got something greasy on my hands. At the station, Whizz and I went to the bathroom to see what was on our hands. I could see several spots of grease on the front of my shirt. It had the smell of Vaseline. The captain came in the bathroom where we were and we showed him the spots on our shirts.

I had washed my hands but they still felt greasy. We went back out on patrol, but things were quiet. The rest of the week was quiet, and the incident was forgotten. But just when everything seem to get back to normal, we got another call to Pennington Avenue.

The Whizz was driving this time and when we stopped in front of the house I got out slowly, looking the place over. Nothing was moving. Then the front door of the house opened, and a woman and a young girl came out screaming, "He is in the house."

I went through the front door just as he came from the bedroom. He made a run at me and I sidestepped him and put a neck hold on him. He slipped out of my hands as if I didn't have a hold of him. The Whizz grabbed him and down on the floor they went. He came up like a greased monkey.

We stood face to face. I have never seen a look on anyone's face like he had. I moved to a position where he couldn't get by me to the door. I rushed him just as Whizz grabbed him again. Then he slid out of Whizz hands and he hit me in the stomach with his head.

He ran into the bedroom and we cornered him before he could shut the door. I reached over and pulled the sheet off the bed. Holding it in front of me, I began to advance on him. He ran toward Whizz and I threw the sheet over him. He went to the floor with my 190 pounds on top of him. That took the fight out of him.

We got him to his feet and tried to cuff him. He had so much grease on him that I wrapped the sheet around him and we carried him to the police station that way.

We got him to the station and he became a totally different person. I recognized him as being the boy who rode the bicycle wearing swim trunks and red tennis shoes. He began to tell me that we had no right to touch him. He carried on and we knew he was sick and didn't need to be in jail.

We left a report telling the day shift what the problem was. They carried him out to the hospital the next day. I found out that he wore the Vaseline on his body to keep anyone from touching him. The Whizz and I found out — you may have touched him but you could not hold him.

Lonie Adcock of Rome is a retired Rome Police Department lieutenant. His latest book is "Fact or Fiction."

GUEST COLUMN: The ghost in the outhouse

Posted: Wednesday, June 29, 2016 6:00 am

Anyone who used an outhouse in the old days will know that it would be the last place a ghost would live. In the summertime an outhouse was not a pleasant place to spend time.

As I have stated in previous stories, when I was growing up I was a very mischievous boy. I realize that some things I did that was fun to me, the other person didn't get a laugh from it.

One such incident was the rigging-up of the outhouse.

When we lived on Reece Street I had put a lot of work on our outhouse. It was probably the most modern one in the neighborhood. I had put all the modern conveniences that could be put into an outhouse. After seeing that people were using an excuse to see the inside, I decided to do something to have some fun.

At that time, we were building a swimming pool on West Third Street. A lot of fishing cord had been used to lay out the foundation. This was the type of cord that fishermen used

Lonie Adcock

Lonie Adcock of Rome is a retired Rome Police Department lieutenant. His latest book is "Fact or Fiction."

on trot lines. I rolled up some of the cord and took it home with me. Then I got some beeswax and, when no one was at home but me, made me a telephone out of tin cans.

I am sure all kids remember making a telephone out of cans and a wax cord. I tied one end to the rear of the outhouse and brought the other end though a window in my bedroom. I took an oatmeal box and made a small hole though the bottom. I pulled the cord though the hole. When you pulled the box, the cord made a low growling noise.

I was all set but didn't know if my telephone and noise-making was going to work. I talked to a buddy of mine and he came down to the house. He went in the outhouse and I began to talk over my makeshift telephone. He waved, letting me know that the telephone worked. I then gave the oatmeal box a pull. He started toward the house laughing. I met him on the porch, and he told me that if the telephone didn't get them, the oatmeal box would.

I was all set. All I had to do was wait for the right time. My sister lived next door to us and the one outhouse was used by both families. My sister had a daughter that I always called Little Sister. She was several years younger than me. She was always having girlfriends who would spend the weekend with her.

I had almost forgotten about rigging the outhouse. It was a Saturday night after we had been ghost hunting with a carload of girls and boys, and I got in kind of late. I eased into the house and in bed without my mother waking up. It was in the summertime and the night was hot and humid. The only kind of cool air you had back then came in through the window. My bed sat in front of the window so that I could get the full benefit of what air came in.

I awoke to hear someone giggling. I rolled over and looked out the window. I saw two girls standing in front of the outhouse. The moon was shining bright and it was easy to see Little Sister and one of her friends. The door of the outhouse was shut, so that meant there was one inside. I reached down beside the bed and picked up the can. I let out a big "ohhhhh."

The door flew open and a voice from in the outhouse asked, "Did you hear that?" Of course the two standing outside hadn't heard anything. I heard the girls tell the one in the outhouse, "Don't be silly. There no one here but us." I reached down and gave the oatmeal box a pull on the waxed cord. The sound that went through the night scared me, until I realized what it was.

I know that you have heard the lion roar at the beginning of some movies. The sound was like a lion roaring.

A scream came from the outhouse and the door came open. A person came out, trying to run and pull up her clothes at the same time. The others girls were already going up the back steps to the house. I sure was glad that my mother was a heavy sleeper, for if she hadn't been I am sure that my laughter would have woke her.

The two other girls were standing with the door open, hollering for the one in the yard to come on. I grew quiet and listened as my sister came to the back porch to see what was going on. I lay still, not making a sound as my sister came down the steps and started toward the outhouse. She opened the door and shined a light inside. She closed the door and went back to the steps and started up.

Then, as if she knew what had happened, she turned and looked straight at the window. I dared not move for the light from the moon lit up my window. She saw me and pointed her finger. I knew that I was in for it the next day. I watched as she and the girls went inside and closed the door. I couldn't help it but had another good laugh before going to sleep.

I slept late the next morning and was sitting at the table eating when I felt a hand on my shoulder. I turned and looked into the face of my sister. "Morning, Sis," I said. She picked up a cup and began to pour a cup of coffee.

"What's up Sis," I asked. She sat down at the table and gave me that big sister know-it-all look. I didn't say anything else, just kept on eating. "I went down and checked out the outhouse this morning, found your ghost." I must have had a smile on my face that ran from ear to ear. "You ought to be ashamed to scare the girls the way you did," she said. Then she began to smile. Then we both began to laugh.

I forgot that I still had the waxed cord on the outhouse until one day I started to go to it and was beat to the door by a neighbor whom I will call Maude. Maude would come down from her house just to use our outhouse. She would always say, "Thank you, it smelled so good."

This time it made me unhappy for I needed the outhouse bad. I grabbed the night pot and used it. I sat on the side of the bed waiting for Maude to come out. Then I saw the can laying on the floor and picked it up. I made a grunting sound into the can.

Nothing happened. I then made a sound like someone with an upset stomach. Nothing, not a sound came from the outhouse. I grabbed the oatmeal box and gave it a pull. A scream and the door came open with Maude running, trying to get her clothes up. I ran to the back porch just as Maude made the road. She went into the road running with her bottom shining.

I looked over at the porch of my sister's house to see her standing there. She just shook her head and went back inside.

Several of my friends in the park asked me if my outhouse was haunted. I would smile and ask, "Where in the world did you hear that?" The smile came from remembering Maude's big fat bottom as she went into the road, pulling at her clothes.

We were never bothered by Maude ever again.

Lonie Adcock of Rome is a retired Rome Police Department lieutenant. His latest book is "Fact or Fiction."

GUEST COLUMN: A dog named Jake

Posted: Wednesday, July 13, 2016 6:00 am

Lonie Adcock

When I was growing up my mother always had a dog, except for one period of time. This was when we moved to Fourth Ward, on the short end of West Ninth Street. Her dog had died and she had not got another one. This is about a dog that won the whole family's hearts, but one that we could not have.

The short end of West Ninth Street is the area where the transmission shop is. At that time, there was one house there. There were others around it, but the one house sat in what was called The Field. If someone asked me where we lived, I would say "in The Field" and everyone in the area knew where I was talking about.

I would leave for school at about 7 o'clock and meet with a crowd of kids to walk to the Neeley School that sat at the foot of the Clock Tower. This was a long walk. We would climb the hill, and by the time you got to school you were ready to sit down for a while. Going down the hill wasn't quite as hard.

Lonie Adcock of Rome is a retired Rome Police Department lieutenant. His latest book is "Fact or Fiction."

On this particular day, I was coming down the hill with a couple of kids when we saw him sitting on the corner of East First Street and East Fifth Avenue. I thought then, and still do, that he was the prettiest dog I had ever seen.

He wagged his tail and came over to me. Now I have always been leery about touching a strange dog. I backed up and he stopped and sat down. I reached and touched him. He licked my hand. I then gave him a loving pat and turned and started on down the hill with my two friends. I never looked back to see where he went.

When I started up the steps to my house, he ran by me and sat down on the top step. I stopped and stared for I had no idea that he had followed me. My only thought was that my mother would skin me alive for bringing home a dog that did not belong to me. He sat there looking at me, wagging his tail. I scratched his head and went into the house.

I tried to explain to my mother what had happened. We walked out on the porch. He came over to her and sat down and held out his paw as if to shake hands. My mother took his paw and scratched his head. He lay down and rolled over for her. I could tell that he had won her heart.

We talked about the fact that he didn't belong to us. That evening I went through the neighborhood to see if

I could find his owner. He walked by my side. When I talked to someone he would sit and look as if he knew what we were talking about. I gave up and went back home. I sat down in ithe front porch and he jumped up beside me, laying his head in my lap. He had won my heart also.

I had noticed that he had on a leather collar with what looked liked diamonds in it. I moved the collar around his neck and found a metal plate on it. There was the name "Jake," and some numbers. I called for my mother and showed it to her. I called him Jake and his ears stood up. I know now that the numbers were a telephone number. Back then, poor folks didn't have a house full of telephones. If we saw a telephone it was in some kind of business.

My mother went back into the house and Jake laid his head in my lap and slept while I read a book.

The next morning when I started to school we let Jake out.

He had slept on my feet that night. At the foot of the steps he stopped and watched me head to where I met the other kids. Jake turned and went back to the swing and lay down. That was the longest day I have ever seen. I thought school would never get out.

I almost ran all the way home, for I wanted to see if Jake was still there. I got to where I could see the house and saw him standing at the top of the stairs. Then he saw me and came running. I played with him, then I went though the neighborhood again trying to find the owner. A Mister Jackson who ran a fruit stand in the neighborhood said he thought he had seen the dog somewhere before.

A week went by and no one came to claim Jake. On Saturday morning two buddies, Jimmy and Robert, came by to see if I wanted to go fishing. With a cane pole and a cup of worms, we headed for the river with Jake by my side. I went to my favorite catfish hole and tossed a hook with a big red worm into the water. The cork went under and I gave a yank. He was a nice one. I got him out on the bank and begin to unwind my stringer.

The fish was flopping around on the ground. Jake walked over and put his nose close to it. If you have ever caught a catfish, you know how they will flop around. Just as Jake got his nose close to the fish it made a flop, hitting him on the nose. He let out a yelp and ran backward. I started to laugh. Jake didn't think it was funny. He began to ease up on the fish again. Just as he got close, the old catfish showed what he could do. It came up off the ground about a foot high. Jake let out a yelp and ran behind me.

Later, Jake and I was sitting in the porch swing when a car pulled into the yard. It was one of those big long ones that all poor boys wanted to own. The driver got out wearing one of those $100 suits that a poor boy could never own. He walked up to the step and said, "I believe that dog there beside you belongs to me." My heart fell and a feeling of nausea came to my stomach. He had come for my Jake.

I realized that Jake didn't belong to me. My mother came out on the porch and the man explained how Mister Jackson had called and told him he thought his dog was here. Jake had got as close to me as he could when the man began to talk. "Jake come here," the man said. Jake raised his head and looked at him then laid his head back in my lap. My heart was breaking for Jake looked as if to say, "Please don't make me go with him."

I could do nothing as the man hooked a leash to his collar. Jake would not get up, so he had to pick him up. He almost fell as he carried him down the steps. He placed him on the back seat. As he pulled off, all I could see was the face of Jake looking out the back glass. My mother went back into the house and I had a good cry.

I thought that I had seen the last of Jake. As the week passed, I missed him but grew to accept that Jake was gone. Jimmy and Robert came by on Saturday and we headed for the Mighty Coosa to wet a few hooks. I would throw my line in the water and smile, remembering Jake and the catfish. We caught a few fish then went home.

As I got close to the house I could not believe my eyes. There, laying in the swing, was Jake. I ran to get to him. He met me and we rolled in the grass, playing. My mother came out and, shaking her head, said, "I told Mister Jackson to call and tell that man his dog was back over here."

It wasn't long before he pulled into the yard. Again he had to carry Jake out to the car. I watched as the car went out of sight with Jake looking out the back glass.

I never saw Jake again. His owner had explained to my mother that Jake was a show dog. He had taken Jake all over the world and Jake had won a lot of money for him. To Jake's owner he was money; to me he was a warm loving creature that God put on this earth to bring happiness to people. They made a piece of equipment out of him and all he wanted was to be a member of some family. Instead of being in a show for money, he wanted to be out playing with a group of kids or fishing with someone who loved him.

I have had a lots of dogs since then, but Jake will always be a part of my memory.

Lonie Adcock of Rome is a retired Rome Police Department lieutenant. His latest book is "Fact or Fiction."

GUEST COLUMN: Do you believe in ghosts ... now?

Posted: Wednesday, July 27, 2016 6:00 am

You walk into a room full of people, look around and find a seat. You shuffle through your papers for the story you will read tonight. The room is buzzing with voices. You begin a study of faces, smiling to yourself. You listen to others read their stories, then your name is called and it's your turn to go to the front of the room.

Everyone is watching, then out of the blue you ask, "How many of you believe in ghosts?" Not a sound is heard. "Come on," you say. Then, over in the corner, a hand goes up. You smile and say, "Only one?" Slowly hands start to rise, until about half of the people in the room admit it.

You smile and say, "I will read you a true story, and then I'll ask again."

Lonie Adcock

Lonie Adcock of Rome is a retired Rome Police Department lieutenant. His latest book is "Fact or Fiction."

A few years back, when I was a teenager, some friends and I would take a carload of girls and go ghost hunting. We went anywhere there were supposed to be ghosts.

This story started when a friend of mine was told about a drive-in theater between Kingston and Cartersville. Finding us a couple of girls, we went in search of the drive-in.

As we went past Kingston we saw two houses that sat off the road. They were empty and we could see that the doors were open. I told my buddy Duke, "I bet we could round us up a ghost in those houses."

I had been told as a kid that they were used as a hospital during the Civil War. The girls didn't want anything to do with ghosts so, for the time being, I let it ride. We found the drive-in and pulled though a driveway under a sign that said S&K Drive In. This was like nothing that I had ever seen.

The movie hadn't started, so Duke and I decided to go get some cokes. This was a hot, muggy, night and a cold drink tasted good. When we stepped out of the car, the grass came up to our knees. They needed to cut their grass, we laughed as we went to the concession stand. With the cokes, back to the car, we waited for the movie to start.

I remember as if yesterday the message that came on the screen. It read "Welcome to the S&K Drive In. This Drive In is like no other that you have ever seen. This is a home folk theater, sit back and enjoy the hospitality of the Sit and Kiss Drive In." We did, way up into the night.

On the way back home, Duke and I began to talk about the houses that we passed just outside of Kingston. Duke pulled down to them when we got to where they were. I got out and walked up on the porch and stood in the doorway. It only took me a few seconds to know that I had found a house to bring the other girls back to. Duke came up on the porch with me. The girls we were with would not get out.

I stepped though the door and into the room. A cold chill went though me and the hair stood up on the back of my neck. I had chill bumps on top of goose bumps. This was definitely a spooky place and our ghost-hunting girls from the park would enjoy these houses. I walked back out on the porch and I heard a voice. I turned to Duke, he shook his head. "That wasn't me you heard," he said.

Going down the steps I would swear that there was someone coming down with us. I got in the car. The girl Myra said, "If I ever go out with you again, you will have to promise me that there will be no visits to abandoned houses." I laughed, saying, "That will never happen."

Return to Kingston

Duke and I talked about getting the ghost-hunting girls together with Carlton and going back up to the houses at Kingston. We didn't like the idea of going close to someone's house, so we decided to ride up to Kingston and talk to someone who lived close by. On Saturday, with Carlton, we headed for Kingston.

There was a house on the same short piece of road that ran by the empty houses. We saw a man sitting on the porch, watching us as we turned into his drive way. I was elected to go up and talk to him. I got out, noticing that his hand was on the inside of his overalls. I walked up and introduced myself. He looked at me in a funny sort of way.

"You not by any chance kin to …" and he called off the name of my grandfather, who was buried in the cemetery there in Kingston. He invited me to sit down and tell him what was on my mind. I explained about the houses and how we had a group that visited haunted houses. He said the houses belonged to him and he didn't let anyone go in them. He knew that people were coming out late at night anyway, and stated that, no matter how many times he closed the door, someone would open it.

He studied me a few minutes and then, to my surprise, said, "Come up tonight at about dark and stop by. I will go with you boys and girls to see if you can stir up a spirit or two." He removed his hand from the front of his overalls to shake hands with me. I saw the handle of a gun inside his overalls. I told him we would be back about dark. I got in to the car and told Duke and Carlton what the old man had in his overall bibs.

I left Duke and Carlton and went home. They would round up our group of Ghost Hunters. It was getting close to dark when they pulled up in front of my house. I went out and squeezed into the back seat. Packed in like sardines, we headed for Kingston. This would be no different from all the others, we thought. But this night would be different in a way that we would never forget.

We pulled up in front of the house and I got out. He met me at the door. "You go ahead," he said. "I will follow you." I got back in to the car and we headed for the houses. It was just a short distance. We got out and waited. Then, from a trail that led from the old man's house, we saw a tractor coming. He was driving his tractor to meet us. He pulled up and, cutting off the motor, began to talk.

He told us some of the history of the houses. They had belonged to a prominent family that owned lots of land in the area. He said that during the war the houses were taken and turned into a hospital. One house was where they were put to get well. The other one was where they were operated on and treated for wounds. He went on to tell how many soldiers had gone through Kingston during the war and the battles that were fought close by. He made it very interesting and we listened, being very quiet.

Then he smiled and said, "You young ones be very careful and don't hurt yourself, and come back some time and tell me about what you saw tonight." He started the tractor and with a wave of his hand, drove back to his house. We watched until he got off of the tractor and went inside. I turned to the others, saying, "Let's go."

I never knew if what the old man had said was true or not. I didn't have any way to check it. We all agreed that he had told us a good story before we went inside the house.

Through the door

I walked up on the porch and stopped in the doorway. I knew then that this was going to be different from all the other ghost hunts we had been on. If you can walk into a house that had all the doors open in 90-degree weather and it feels like an icebox, you know that something is not right. The old chill went down my back and the hair stood up on my arms and the back of my neck.

When I stepped though the door I would have swore at that time I saw someone go in to the next room. I went over and with my pen light, looked the room over. No one was there and there was no door for anyone to have gone out. There were noises all through the house and what sounded like voices in pain.

The girls and Carlton had backed out of the room, onto the front porch, but one, Francis, was still standing by my side with her eyes wide open. I felt someone come up beside me and, turning, I looked into the face of Duke. He said in a quiet voice, "I am with you come hell or high waters." I let him know that I heard him.

I moved toward an open door that led in to a hallway, Duke and Francis with me. I don't think that any of us was prepared for what happened next. A gruff voice said as plain as day, "Put his dead butt on the table." We stood still, for it appeared that there was someone in the room. I stepped though the door and into the room. There was no one there. What looked like a mist was in the far corner. It looked like smoke. I kept moving and could feel Duke and Francis move with me.

Once in the corner, the mist said, "Move, damn it. You are in the way." Was I imagining things? If so, Duke and Francis were also. Their faces told me they were ready to go but would stay if I stayed. I eased back into the hallway. I could see open doors. I wanted to go down the hall, past the room, to see if I could hear anything. And hear things we did.

There was moaning and groaning, sounds like someone was cussing. There was a gruff voice that seemed to be trying to push us out of the house. The doors began to slam and that was all that it took.

I headed for the back door with Duke and Francis on my heels. I reached the back porch and down the steps in nothing flat. I was chilled to the bone but sweat was running down my face and into my eyes. I looked at

Duke and Francis. "Want to go back though the house, or around it?" We all agreed — around it.

The others were standing beside the car waiting for us. They all gathered around us. Then I remember saying, "All right you chickens, gather close, for we all are going back into the house." I started to laugh when I saw the looks on their faces. Then, from out of nowhere, a deep laugh sounded from inside the house. I quickly opened the door and jumped in the back seat.

And I remember laughing until tears ran down my cheeks at them trying to get into the car.

Looking back

We talked about this for days to come. We would sit in the park and try to find an answer for what we had seen and heard. Were there ghosts in the old houses from the war days? Was we set up by the old man who owned the houses? Did he decide to have some fun out of a bunch of young people?

If the old man had set it up, he did a good job. If he didn't, then whatever was in the old house did even a better job.

Did I mention that it felt like someone was walking in the house with us, smoking a cigar? One thing that Duke, Francis and I agreed on was that there was someone in there with us smoking a cigar. The cigar smoke smell stayed in our clothes until they were washed,

I never got back to talk to the old gentleman who owned the houses. A fellow by the name of Uncle Sam put a hitch in my plans for several years. When I got back, there were no longer a bunch of ghost hunters left. Some were married, some had moved off.

It was a different place that I came back to. I was a different person after my Uncle Sam got though with me.

You look around the room and again ask, "How many of you now believe in ghosts?"

Lonie Adcock of Rome is a retired Rome Police Department lieutenant. His latest book is "Fact or Fiction."

GUEST COLUMN: Some police calls I'll never forget

Posted: Wednesday, August 3, 2016 6:00 am

Here's a story about police calls and some funny things I ran up on.

One day I was turning off of East Second Avenue onto Glen Milner when I noticed a car pulled over to the side of the road. As I approached the car I could not believe what I saw. Two men were in the front, slugging it out.

Fists were flying and the language was awful to hear. I called for backup and got out of the car.

The big fellow had the little one on the hood, banging his head against it. I got the two separated and tried to find out what was the problem.

It seemed like every time the little fellow had beans for dinner he would get in the car and lay a few stinkys on his buddy. The big man was almost crying while telling me what it smelled like in his car, when the little fellow popped another.

Lonie Adcock

Lonie Adcock of Rome is a retired Rome Police Department lieutenant. His latest book is "Fact or Fiction."

The other patrol car pulled up in time to hear the big fellow's story. We both were laughing so hard that it was hard for us to hear all of it.

I thought I would give the little fellow a chance to tell his side of the story. He said all his wife knew how to cook were pinto beans. He said that he ate a big bowl of beans with onions and they would put gas on his stomach. He looked so solemn when he said, "Once the gas is in there, the only place for it to go is out."

I told them to get in the car and behave themselves. They assured me they would. I got back in the patrol car, giving them time to pull out in front of me.

Just as the car crossed the railroad track it came to a stop. The doors came open and here the two went at it again.

I called the other patrol car back and we loaded them up and carried them to the station. I put the little fellow in the officer's car and the big fellow in mine.

I laughed all the way to the station, listening to him tell about the little fellow and his stinkers.

At the police station I told the jailer to put them in the same cell.

As I was leaving, going back out on patrol, I heard the big fellow saying, "Officer have mercy, don't put us in the cell together." I always wondered how it worked out, the two of them in the same cell.

I remember another call that has stayed with me down though the years. A call came for a car to check on a house on East Fifth Avenue. I was close and told dispatch that I would back up the car. We pulled in front of the house at the same time and walked up to the front door.

We listened for a few minutes before knocking. Then I knocked and stepped to the side of the door.

We could hear someone moving about inside. The door slowly opened and a woman peeped out. I identified us and she opened the door saying, "Come on in. Maybe you can talk some sense into the old idiot."

She looked to be in her early 60s, and he looked to be in his late 70s. I noticed when I came through the door that he was missing a leg. It was his right leg.

Her story went like this: "Every Saturday night he goes down to Mae's place on South Broad and throws away his money on the floozies at that joint." She said that he was crazy about some old bar bat with red hair.

He would drink up his money and give the old bat at the joint a good time.

When he got polluted, he came home smelling like a beer keg and crawled into bed with her. He would go to sleep with a foul breath. She had to sleep on the couch because he smelled so bad. "I fixed him tonight," she said. "I hid his crutches and he will have to stay at home and not see his bar babies."

I saw the problem when she said she hid his crutches.

I could see that without them he could not go anywhere. I looked at him to see if he wanted tell his side of the story.

He looked at me and, with a wink, asked, "Did you take a look at that old hag? I sit here every night listening to her. I like to go out and have a beer, play the machines and shoot the bull with my buddies."

She had turned red in the face and I could see what was about to happen. I interrupted before she could say anything. "Why don't you take her with you some night and let her see how much fun you are having and maybe she will join you," I said. They let out a "WHAT?" at the same time. I knew that there wasn't anything I could say that would make the two quiet down.

I left with the warning that if we had to come back someone would go to jail. We didn't have any more calls that night. I often wondered if she hid his crutches every Saturday night in order to keep him at home.

Here is another one for you: A call was given to a patrol car that a man was running through Myrtle Hill Cemetery without any clothes. I had no intentions of getting involved in this chase. I pulled into where you go down to Coosa Country Club. I turned facing Myrtle Hill. I could see the officers walking and looking for the subject.

Then, from out of nowhere, he jumped up on a tombstone and let out a yell. The officers scrambled down the hill, trying to get to him. He disappeared from sight.

I sat in the cool car laughing at the officers scrambling around.

The laugh was short-lived when he came running up in front of the patrol car. He bent over and patted his rear end at me. I started to get out of the car. He turned and ran toward the river.

Just as I got to where I could see him, he jumped into the river. I called all the cars, telling them that he was swimming across the river behind the levee.

As I watched, he climbed out of the river and headed toward the railroad on the levee. He ran over the levee just as a car came though the floodgate — over the levee and into the emergency room at the hospital.

I didn't go to the hospital but found out later that he was treated and moved out to Northwest Georgia Regional Hospital.

Lonie Adcock of Rome is a retired Rome Police Department lieutenant. His latest book is "Fact or Fiction."

GUEST COLUMN: Beanie, cowboys and dreams of hard work

Posted: Wednesday, August 17, 2016 6:00 am

Back in my school days I had a boy in my class that everyone called Beanie. Beanie's real name was Charles. I never called him Beanie. I have always thought that to tag someone with a nickname was the worst thing that you could do. I remember a boy from school who was tagged Burr Head by his father. It was still with him all though life.

Beanie wasn't the smartest boy in class. Everyone thought he was the dumbest — everyone but me. I knew that Beanie was a dreamer. He would sit and his mind would be floating around somewhere in outer space. I did some of that in my younger days. I would read a good book and take a journey to some country that had flying carpets and Knights of the Round Table.

Lonie Adcock

Lonie Adcock of Rome is a retired Rome Police Department lieutenant. His latest book is "Fact or Fiction."

Where I dreamed of different things, Beanie dreamed of sailing the oceans blue. I used to laugh and ask him if he was part fish. His face would turn red and he would get quiet. I think I was the only friend that he had in school. If you talked to him and didn't know, you would get the idea he was slow. But he was a smart boy, when you got down and talked to him.

Beanie's clothes stood him out among other kids. He wore clothes that looked like what sailors wore. A blue scarf was always around his neck. His family was well off, so he could wear any kind of clothes. I wore my overalls and tennis shoes. I can imagine what people thought when two boys about the same age came by, one in a sailor outfit and the other in overalls and a pullover shirt.

And Beanie could not play games like other kids — his had to be a Navy game. I remember him in grade school and into high school. When he finished high school, he enlisted in the Navy. Many years later I saw him, and he had stripes of rank and medals to show that he had worked hard.

As a kid, mine were cowboy games, and I could ride with the best there was. I would wind up outshooting the bad guys and putting them in jail. After a Saturday in the movies watching the good guys, I could put myself in the place of the cowboys. Kids back in those days dreamed about different things than those of today.

I kept the cowboy dream for quite a while. Then, after a visit to my half-brother, it went down the drain. My half-brother's son Weldon and I went out to the pasture to take a ride on an old mule used to plow the garden. Weldon got pulled off by riding under a limb on a tree. I hit the ground when he came to a sudden stop.

I was lying under him, with his foul breath blowing in my face. When I would move, trying to get from under him, he would let out a whinny and move with me. I must have slid halfway across that pasture on my back, trying to get from under and away from his foul breath. Then he let go with water pouring from his back end.

I took off running with everything I had in me. He let out another whinny and started after me. I went between the wire on the fence just as he tried to take a nip out of me. He missed and I jumped to my feet saying ugly words to him.

I saw Weldon lying on the ground under the tree and ran around the fence, trying to get to him. I began to call Weldon and he finally sat up. I heard a whinny and here came the old mule running toward him. He jumped up, running as fast as he could. He came though the wire in the fence just as the old mule grabbed the seat of his pants. He jerked loose and sat on the ground, saying ugly words to the old mule.

It didn't bother the old mule. He let out another whinny and went running out across the pasture. I never really thought about riding a horse to chase bad guys any more.

When I got grown, I knew that chasing the bad guys in an air-conditioned car was a lot better. I became a police officer instead of a cowboy.

Another of my dreams was to write a book of short stories. I started back in the 1960s playing around with a typewriter. I did some stories but never got them published. They are boxed up in my basement. I am going to pull them out and see what they sound like now.

Now if you have more than one dream, pick the one you want the most. Pursue it, and then when you are finished, you can start on another one. I do not believe that you get too old to pursue a dream. There is a possibility that if you dream about the blonde around the corner you can forget it, unless you have made a million dollars. … You'd better make that $2 million, with today's prices.

There are all kind of people in all walk of life who have dreams. Some will get out and work for their dream and make it come true. Others will walk around and complain about the way things are. Others want to ride the free programs. I am of the belief that if you want to do something, do it. Make up the mind and the body will follow.

To the young I say if you have a dream, go for it. When you are young you can pursue many paths in life. If you find that you are on the wrong road then do some tall thinking, gather your thoughts, and go for your new dream. Just because things don't seem to work out right the first time, you try and try again. If you stay with it long enough you can make it come true.

To those in my age group, throw away the beer and push those peanuts back, get out of that chair if possible. Go and join a senior program and get with people and enjoy life. My wife and I belong to the Georgia Mountain Music Club. We look forward to every Wednesday, getting together with our friends from 10 a.m. to noon at the Charles C. Parker Center and listening to some good country music.

There are a lot of good friends you haven't met. Get out and meet them. Enjoy every day that the good lord gives us to the fullest.

I have had a good life. Growing up as a poor boy, it was hard. But I had my dreams and they have come true. I had a good career in law enforcement and I have had five books published. The one thing that I am proudest of is that God gave me a wife who has worked and stood by me in my endeavors. What more can a person ask for? Oh yes, he gave me a good group of friends.

At my age I feel that I have indeed been blessed. May you have a dream, and may it come to you through hard work.

Lonie Adcock of Rome is a retired Rome Police Department lieutenant. His latest book is "Fact or Fiction."

GUEST COLUMN: Strange questions, not-so-strange answers

Posted: Monday, August 22, 2016 3:30 pm

I recall some things that I saw people do that seemed odd. Having no knowledge why they were doing these things got my curiosity up. So I would ask them. Got some strange answers. As a young fellow, it seemed strange to see a grown up doing things that didn't make sense to me.

When I was a kid going to Neely School, I had to walk from Fourth Ward to Rome's Clock Tower Hill. There was this man who walked the street looking for pieces of string. You could see him all over town, walking and looking at the street. He would pick up the string and take a roll from a bag that he had on his shoulder. He would tie the piece he had found to the roll and then place it back into his shoulder bag.

Lonie Adcock

Lonie Adcock of Rome is a retired Rome Police Department lieutenant. His latest book is "Fact or Fiction."

I also remember a man who walked the street picking up cigarette packs. He would straighten out the pack and then fold it and place it with others that he had. He would take the aluminum foil and fold it and place it with others that he had. You might see him just about anywhere you went in town. He carried what look like a briefcase with him to put the aluminum in. I watched him place the pack separately from the foil.

Then there was a man who carried a sack and picked up bottle caps. I have seen him with the sack so full that he could hardly walk. When you saw him he would be walking in the gutter. I was told by my mother to never walk in the gutter for you could be hit by a car. He didn't seem to care, for in the gutter was where the bottle caps were.

As a police officer, I remember answering a call to a clothing store on Broad Street. When I got there the salesman told me to watch a woman who was looking at a blouse. I watched as she looked the blouse over, then wrote in a notebook. She then moved over to another table and did the same thing. I thought at the time that this was odd.

Back in the old days, cars were not as plentiful as today. I remember that I would catch the bus at Callahan and North Broad. There was this fellow who would watch as the bus passed, going to where it turned around. Then he would start to walk at a fast pace. He worked at a service station at the corner of Sixth and Broad. I would look for him, and most of the time he would be almost at work when we passed him.

There also was this fellow who would walk down Broad Street talking to himself. I would stand and watch him and wonder what he was saying. Sometimes he would be talking to himself and burst out laughing. I often wondered what someone could say to himself that would make you laugh at yourself.

Then there was a town drunk who would come up to me on the street. I would look at him and say, "Go and sleep it off." In return, he would blow his foul breath in my direction and say, "I am drunk and demand to be locked up." I remember telling him, to go away for I didn't have time to mess with him. I'd say, "Come back when the traffic dies down." He would go into a back alley but reappear when the traffic died down. I would call a car and send him to jail.

Let's go back and see if there was a good reason for what these people were doing.

Take the man who walked around picking up string. I approached him and asked him what he did with the string. He said that another man had a roll of string that weighed a record-breaking amount. His goal was to beat it and make a Guinness World Record of his. Sounded logical to me.

What about the man who walked around picking up cigarette packs? He told me that the tobacco company gave away prizes for a certain number of packs, along with the aluminum foil. He showed me a pocket knife and, smiling, he said, "I got this for only 500 packs and foil." Sounded okay to me — for at that time, there was no way of beating having a good pocket knife.

There was the man who went around with a sack on his back picking up bottle caps. As a small boy, I approached him out of curiosity. He smiled as I handed him a bottle cap. I remember asking him why he wanted them. He had a folder and he opened it. There were pictures of all the old cowboys. My eyes must have bugged out, for he had a smile a mile long on his face when he said you could trade them for movie tickets. Well, I'm here to tell you that I cut into his business, for I kept all the bottle caps that I could find. To a small boy who loved westerns, it made good sense to collect bottle caps.

I remember approaching the woman in the clothing store rather hesitantly. She smiled and said, "Officer, how are you?" I explained why I was there and that the people who owned the store were wondering what she was doing. It was quite simple when she said, "Comparing prices with other stores." She would go around comparing prices, then go back and buy the one with the best price. Nothing wrong with her, a thrifty shopper.

There was the man looked like he was trying to outwalk the bus. I asked him one morning what he was doing. He smiled and said, "Saving money. I let the bus get even with me, then start to walk. The bus goes to the end of the line and by the time he gets back to pick me up, I can get within a block of my work. That saves a nickel. In a week I have saved a quarter. It's all about saving money." I guess it's good to be thrifty, but from Callahan to where I had to go it was well worth a nickel.

There was the fellow who walked Broad Street talking to himself. I watched him and one day I asked him why, and what he found funny. He looked at me and said, "Officer, I get to the point to where I want to talk to someone with some sense, so I talk to myself. And as far as me laughing, I sometimes tell myself a joke that I have never heard." Letting out a big laugh, he turned and headed down the street. I knew I had been had. Laughing to myself, I went into the street and worked traffic.

And the old drunk — the reason he wanted to go to jail? The jail was the only home he knew. It was a place to sleep and be fed. He would get a check, and when his money ran out that meant no more booze He would live in jail until the next check came. Nothing wrong with him. Just a case of survival.

Lonie Adcock of Rome is a retired Rome Police Department lieutenant. His latest book is "Fact or Fiction."

GUEST COLUMN: Before finding fault with others, stop and take a look at yourself

Posted: Wednesday, August 31, 2016 6:00 am

In my 86 years I have known a lot of people. It is very seldom that I have found two people exactly alike. And a person's appearance doesn't always reflect their mind. Growing up as a skinny boy, wearing overalls and tennis shoes, made me a target for bullying. That is, until they found out that I carried a big stick and would use it.

Here are a few stories about people who were different.

Several years back I wrote a book for kids ages 9 to 90 called "Elmer the Dancing Turtle." Ma and Pa Turtle's hearts swelled with pride as they watched a little boy turtle and then a little girl turtle crack out of their eggs. It seemed an eternity before the third egg moved, then out came a little boy turtle — dancing. His mother and father knew Elmer was different from the others. He was accepted by his family, but how would the rest of the world accept him?

This brings me back to a girl that I went to school with. I will not call her real name. I will call her Skippy, the name that the kids gave her.

Skippy was a very pretty girl but she skipped along when she should have walked. She always seemed to be full of energy. She would start out walking and end up skipping. It looked like she was jumping rope.

The idea of a dancing Turtle came from Skippy. Those that knew Skippy loved her, for she was a very sweet caring person. There was a wall at Elm Street School that we would sit on during recess. She would see me sitting on the wall and come over and sit with me. I had many a child's conversation with her.

When we moved from West Rome and changed school, I lost sight of her. But I ran across her later at an Easter egg hunt. Though years had passed since seeing her, she was the same caring person as when she was Skippy. She grew into a pretty girl. Oh yes, and she still skipped.

Then there was a boy who was in my class for three years. He and I were the best of friends. His name was Walter, but due to a defect in his left foot, he limped. The bigger boys gave him the name Limpy.

Limpy was overweight. I believe it was because he could not run and play as others did. He would sit on the wall with a few of us. I never called him Limpy for I was taught never to make fun of other's misfortune.

Limpy was born with his defect and no one could change that. Being at a disadvantage, he turned to something he could do. His interest was in electronics. He would tear down radios and any kind of electronic equipment he could find. He later went to school to learn electronics. He became a radio and television repair man. He was one of the best in the area at one time.

He was different because he was overweight and walked with a limp. Did he deserve the names he was called as a kid? He had a good mind and put it to work for himself in later years. I do not believe that anyone should be subject to name-calling.

There was a lady who lived on the street behind me when I lived in Fourth Ward. Her first name was Evie. All the kids in the neighborhood called her "Crazy Evie." All the kids except the Adcocks. When we met her we called her Miss Eve, and her face would light up.

Miss Eve was getting old and her yard would grow up. She had a hard time keeping the grass cut. I saw her trying to cut the grass and I told my mother that I was going to help her. I walked up to her and told her to let me see the lawn mower. I began to cut the grass.

Her yard wasn't too big, so it didn't take very long. Miss Eve had a fenced-in garden. It was full of tomatoes and other garden stuff. When I got though, I left and went fishing with a couple of buddies. I got back and there was a table full of vegetables. Miss Eve had got them out of her garden and brought them to us.

I had caught a big mess of catfish that day. Seeing Miss Eve in her garden, I went to the fence and called to her. She came over and I asked her if she liked fish. He eyes lit up and she said "Henry used to catch fish and we would eat them. I haven't had fish in a long time." I gave the fish to her. With a thank you, she took the fish and went into the house.

"Crazy Evie," as folks called her, was one of the best people in the neighborhood. She was a very old woman who was lonesome. When we made friends with her she showed us what a friend could be. If one of us got sick, Miss Eve was the first one there to help out. Take time to know people before you tag them with a name.

I left most of my school friends when we moved from West Rome. My first year at Neely I met and made new friends. There was a boy named Austin. Even as long as it has been, I do believe that he was the ugliest boy that I ever met.

Austin may have been ugly but he was one of the most decent people that I have ever met. I was standing on the steps on the first day of school when a boy standing close said, "Well, well, here come old Pug Ugly." I saw who he was talking about, and admitted to myself that he was uglier than I was. I still didn't believe that gave anyone to right to call him Pug Ugly.

Time went on and I noticed that Austin would stay by himself. I decided to make friends with him. I would sit on a bench where he sat and start a conversation with him. It wasn't long before he was walking home with us.

The crowd of boys and girls that walked from Fourth Ward to Neely never called him Pug Ugly. We all called him Austin. His name. He finally felt that our group was his friends and we weren't going to make fun of him. He fit in, and being ugly didn't bother him.

Now he may have been ugly back then, but Austin married a girl who was a beauty. If you stop and think about it — age will make you look better or worse. Austin looked better as he aged. I have always believed the good Lord made us the way he wanted us to look.

My last words are: Before you find fault with others, stop and look at yourself. Then, if you are perfect, you may call others names.

Lonie Adcock of Rome is a retired Rome Police Department lieutenant. His latest book is "Fact or Fiction."

COLUMN: But it didn't take long for me to fit in ...

Posted: Wednesday, September 14, 2016 6:00 am

This story started the day I was born. That was 86 years ago. I can sit back and see the different periods of time go by.

I grew up in the 1930s and '40s, going to the cotton fields with my father. He was a sharecropper farmer. After he had his crop in, he would work with the people who had larger farms.

I remember seeing the hogs hanging from tree limbs and the people working on them. He would help at hog-killing time for the meat. I can remember when he would bring home buckets of sorghum syrup. Again, he helped make syrup and got paid in buckets. If you had food and a place to live back then, you were lucky.

Then farming — like everything else — got bad. The landowners asked for more of the crop. It was hard to get a piece of land that was big enough. The landowners cut the size that they shared. That made less for the man who was farming the land.

Lonie Adcock

Lonie Adcock of Rome is a retired Rome Police Department lieutenant. His latest book is "Fact or Fiction."

My last year living on the farm was in a house at the end of the Hardin Bridge. The house sat between the river and the road at the end of the bridge crossing on the right from Kingston. I remember hearing my mother and father talk about moving to town. I was so small that I didn't know the difference between town and country. I soon found out.

In the country we had our fish hole on the river. We had all kind of playing area. There was no one else but the family. My father ran into an old friend who offered him a job in construction. The next thing I remember, we moved to what was called Wright Row; it is now called John Davenport Drive.

We lived there until the spring rains came. The creek that ran though the woods below us got up into the house. After it went down, we moved to Armstrong Street that ran off of Allen Street. Armstrong, since those days, has ceased to exist. The pipe factory took it in when they built there.

Then I found out about town living. I turned 6 and off to school I went. I remember that I stood out in the crowd. The others wore a different type of clothing. I wore overalls with a red pullover shirt and blue tennis shoes. If you don't think you will stand out with those clothes on, give the little fellow a bowl hair cut.

But it didn't take long for me to fit in. The first year I made a lot of friends. I also met a lot who were not friends. You see that funny-looking skinny boy who took no guff from anyone? Like then, and like it still is, there were little groups that stayed and played together. That was a long time ago. On occasions I will run into someone I went to school with, but they are few and far between. At recess time the wall at the Elm Street School held the same group for about five years.

There was no cotton-picking in the city. There were farmers who came to the city and picked up people and carried them to the cotton field. You would load on a truck and they drove you to the field. The cotton field was a playground for some kids. Back when we went to the cotton fields, it was a work area. Those kids did not have to work for a living.

I went to Neely and then to Rome High — I believe that they called the high school Hill Toppers or something like that. I wanted to play football, but the coach told me I was too small. At that time I weighed about 110 pounds. After being told that I was too small, I never cared anything about football.

Then came the point where I had no choice but to quit school and go to work, at the age of 13. My first job was washing dishes at a cafe. From dishwashing to short order cook. I didn't care for cooking, so I got a job at construction. Worked there until I went into service. I never quit learning, for when I wasn't at work you could find me with a book or a paper of some kind, reading and learning.

We were being processed into the Army and at night had nothing to do. I talked to a sergeant and he let me into the library. There was only material there that pertained to the Armed Forces. I found a book on the Signal Corps and began to read. I did that for several nights. Then came the time for a test to see what branch of service we would be best for. You guessed it — I was put into the Signal Corps. Tell me it don't pay to read.

I came out of the service and a couple of years later went on the Rome Police Department. I walked a beat on Broad Street for a while. Then I was put into a patrol car where I worked until I was promoted to the rank of detective sergeant. From detective I went back on patrol as a sergeant. I was promoted to the rank of lieutenant. I was Watch Commander until retirement.

From hanging hogs in trees and butchering them to now, I have seen a lot of changes. Most of the changes have been for the best, but a lot haven't.

Lonie Adcock of Rome is a retired Rome Police Department lieutenant. His latest book is "Fact or Fiction."

COLUMN: Fun at the old swim hole

Posted: Thursday, September 29, 2016 3:30 pm

I have written stories about the old swim hole before. I remember that we had a swim hole on Horseleg Creek when we were small boys. The mothers would bring us over on the weekend and let us play in the creek.

I now believe that what they were doing was getting us to take a bath. I remember that we always had to soap ourselves down. My mother would let us wear cut-off pants and we were told to pull them back and soap up our bottoms. Now tell me that wasn't a sly way of getting us kids to take a bath.

The creek ran down the mountain behind Shorter College. We had to go down Sherwood Road and go into the woods off the road.

When we would slip off from home, we would go onto the creek bank on Hanks Street. It would take us a little longer to get to the swim hole that way, but no one would see us. The creek ran away from houses in the area then. Now the creek has houses all around it. I was told after they tore the dam down the swim hole went dry, except in rainy weather.

Lonie Adcock

Lonie Adcock of Rome is a retired Rome Police Department lieutenant. His latest book is "Fact or Fiction."

I remember the first time I saw the swim hole it was just a small trickle of water. With the help of the boys in the neighborhood we put rocks across the creek and got about three feet of water in the deepest part. We kids, when with our mothers, had to play in the shallow water. There was a big rock was in the middle of the creek. Some of the boys would get on the rock and dive into the deeper water when the mothers wasn't there.

After a good summer rain, the water would rise and cover the rock in the middle of the creek. If anyone who wasn't familiar with the rock came by, we would sit on it. It would look like the water was about six inches deep.

One day a bunch of us boys slipped off and went to the swim hole. Unknown to us, some of the girls had followed us. When we saw them approach, we decided to have some fun. We got together and sat on the rock. They began to tell us how they were going to tell our mothers on us, for slipping away from home and going in the creek.

We laughed, telling them to wade out to us; that the water would not be over their feet. Then we did the unthinkable — we double dog dared them to wade out.

We knew if they stepped into the water it would come up to their waist. We put on faces that looked like we were scared to death they were going to tell on us. Then we taunted them, saying they were scared of getting their little footsies wet. Oh, we laid it on good.

Finally they sat down and began to pull off their shoes. Then they held hands and stepped into what they thought was shallow water. They hollered like someone had shot them when their dresses floated up on top of the water,

We were having us a high old time laughing at the girls when I noticed one was having a problem. She had lost her footing and was thrashing around in the water. I jumped off the rock and ran to her. I got her on her feet and out of the water. The others was following.

With everyone out of the water and the girls crying about their wet dresses, they began to get on us. That was one time there was a quiet bunch of boys and a loud group of girls. We finally convinced then that their clothes would be dry before that walked back home. From that time on, we kept an eye out for the girls when we slipped off to the swim hole.

Another time, we were at the swim hole with our mothers and family. We all wore cut-off pants. Again, I believe that was our weekly bath. A boy I will call Tooney had come to the swim hole wearing his good clothes. He watched us playing in the water. I could tell that he was miserable and wanted to get in.

I went over to him and told him to go down where the deep water was and come into the water naked. He shook his head, but finally gave in and came in naked. Bushes grew to the creek bank at the deep end. He slid into the water and no one paid any attention to him. In the deep water you could not see that he was naked. We stayed and played in the creek for a long time.

Then … it was apparent that Tooney forgot he was naked. He got up on the rock, bottom shining. He hollered to where everyone looked at him. He did a perfect dive — with his naked bottom shining in the sunlight that seeped through the trees.

The mothers were yelling at him and the rest of us was laughing so hard that tears were running down our cheeks. I saw Tooney as he left the water, grabbing his clothes and running naked through the woods.

Tooney was hard to find for a while after that. It finally was forgotten by the mothers, but we never let him forget. I understand that Tooney was treated for those small bugs that are called chiggers. It was said that, running through the woods naked, he got a good dose of the little red fellows.

Lonie Adcock of Rome is a retired Rome Police Department lieutenant. His latest book is "Fact or Fiction."

GUEST COLUMN: Names I have been called

Posted: Wednesday, October 5, 2016 6:00 am

When you are brought into this world you are given a name by your parents. In later years you may get tagged with a nickname. I was called Burt, after my middle name. I was in school before I found out that my first name was Lonie. Spelled with one N.

I started to school at West Rome Elm Street. The teacher would call other kids to answer questions. I often wondered as I sat there why she didn't call on me. One day she told me to wait after school. She put me in her car and we headed for my house. She sat on the porch and talked to my mother.

Kids back then didn't butt in on any conversation between the older folks. I sat across the porch from them. I could hear them and could make out what they were talking about. She was telling my mother that I was hard of hearing.

My mother looked at me and said, "Burt, come here." I went over to where they were. That was when my teacher found out that I was called Burt. The next day in school when she called me, it was Lonie Burt. I finally accepted Lonie and dropped Burt down to a middle initial.

Lonie Adcock

Lonie Adcock of Rome is a retired Rome Police Department lieutenant. His latest book is "Fact or Fiction."

That was one of the good names that I was called. There were some names that I can not put on paper. If you are a policeman or intend to be one, you might as well get ready, for they will call you all kind of names. When I went on the police department I was called names that I had no idea existed.

One time I was working a bad wreck at Maple and East 12th Street. It was one of those days when the thermometer had reached 100 degrees. After getting the information and clearing the road, I was standing at the back of the patrol car finishing the wreck report.

Two girls came by, they stopped and one of them said something. Not hearing, I said, "Beg your pardon." One laughed and said, "Do you know what policemen are made of?" I shook my head no. Then they laughed and one of them said, "Copper, dirty old copper." They giggled a little and then went on down the street.

I had asked for that one. I should have kept on working my wreck report. I vowed that I would be ready the next time.

Then there was the time a crowd had gathered at the corner of a street. We were sent to move them on because the people who lived on the street were complaining about the language. We moved in and began to disperse the crowd when someone yelled "Pigs!" I had never been called a pig before, so, I tried to find out who had said it. Picking out the one who looked guilty, I said, "Come here, I want to talk to you." I laughed as he ran around the corner of Maple Street.

Later, someone came up that pig stood for Pride, Integrity and Guts.

There was a call that I remember answering where a drunk would take his wife's paycheck and spend it for booze. He sat in a chair, some 250 pounds of him, drinking beer. Two small kids were eating a few saltine crackers from a box. There was no food in the refrigerator or anywhere in the house. The older daughter had gone to stay with kinfolks because of him. I tried to get him outside but he had it pulled on him before. He stayed in the house, knowing that as long as he didn't do anything we could not touch him.

I looked at the cowed-down woman and two kids and my blood pressure went to the boiling point. I went out to the car and called headquarters. I asked that they check the jail to see if they had a warrant for him. In just a few minutes dispatch informed me that the sheriff's car was en route, they had an outstanding warrant for him. I have never been much of a dancer but I know that, with a smile on my face, I must have danced all the way back to the house.

With him on his way to jail, I talked to the lady and we called Family Services and got her some help. She had a job, so everything worked out all right. I soon forgot about it. One day I went to eat with my sergeant at a restaurant. Someone hugged me from behind, saying, "I wanted to see you again to thank you, my Blue Angel." I turned around and it was the lady whom I had helped.

She said her oldest daughter was in college and the other two were doing good in school. As we were getting into the car to leave, my sergeant said, "I have heard you called everything now. I can't believe you are a Blue Angel." I laughed and said, "Be quiet. Don't let anyone else hear about this." Of course, as you can guess, it got all over the department that I was an angel. At least it was good, not a bad thing I was called.

Then came the day I retired — no more name-calling. Wrong. For just after a short time I published a book, "Memories of an Old Geezer." Then someone called me an old codger. Those aren't bad names, for I will admit that I am an old codger. I have also been call an old grump. I don't believe if you look at this face you will call me an old grump. Old, yes. Grump, never.

But it really doesn't matter what you call me if you call when the food is on the table.

Lonie Adcock of Rome is a retired Rome Police Department lieutenant. His latest book is "Fact or Fiction."

GUEST COLUMN: Beckett, Braggs and the hanging crossroad

Posted: Wednesday, October 19, 2016 6:00 am

I tell stories that were told to us kids as we grew up. True or not, they were told to us and we never questioned them. I will tell this one and let you draw your own conclusion.

It is supposed to have happened back in the 1800s in a small community somewhere in the mountains of North Georgia. If you ever run across a place called Beckett Corner, then you will know you are where this story took place.

Beckett came into the community when he inherited a small farm from an uncle. The people gave him the nickname "Slim." Beckett was about 6-foot-6 and his legs were long and skinny. When you looked at him he seemed to be all legs.

At first glance, it looked as if his legs started under his armpits. It was a sight to see, him riding his old mule. His legs almost reached to the ground.

It was said of Beckett that he was a good person. If anyone needed help he would be the first person to lend you a hand. He was well liked in the community, but there was one who did not like him. He was the community bully. His name was Roscoe Braggs.

Lonie Adcock

Lonie Adcock of Rome is a retired Rome Police Department lieutenant. His latest book is "Fact or Fiction."

Roscoe was disliked by most. He was a hellraiser and on Saturday night he made all the bars in the nearby town. Once they were closed he would come back to the community and find someone to pick a fight with. He was always in trouble with the law.

On one occasion he had been out drinking and had a run-in with a sheriff's deputy. He jumped the deputy and knocked him down. The deputy shot him in the leg.

The community was rid of him for a while. But once he got well and served his time, he came back.

Beckett would get up before daylight and get in the fields, plowing. People marveled at this — he had to have a plow special built on account of his height. With his long legs and arms, an everyday plow for most would put him in a stooped-over position.

He would plow until the hot of the evening, then go home and sit in the shade and drink tea. He would go over to the city and get ice and put it in a place that he had built in the basement.

No one knew how he kept the ice from melting, but they knew that if you went by he would give you a cold glass of tea. His tea did not taste like the tea that most of them drank. He called it sassafras tea. No one knew what it was really made of, but a cold glass of it would cool you down.

At holiday gatherings Beckett would drive a wagon to the community center and sell his tea. Braggs had always sold lemonade at the holiday events. Beckett's tea was selling and Braggs was losing money.

Braggs set his lemonade stand up that morning for the Fourth of July celebration. There were all kinds of events to enter. The horseshoe throwing and the checker games were the most popular.

A stage had been set up and the music started. Braggs watched as Beckett's wagon came down the road.

His face grew red and he let out some words that sent people scattering.

They knew Braggs was going to start something with Beckett and a man was sent for the sheriff, but they all knew it would take a while for a deputy to get there. Unknowing of the pending trouble, Beckett unhooked his horse and put him in a place where he could get grass and water. He let down a couple of boards on the side of the wagon. He took a pick handle and drove up some stakes. The planks he let down made a table to serve his tea from.

He lay the pick handle on the tailgate of the wagon and began to sell his tea.

The story goes that Braggs watched the people drinking Becketts tea and began a slow burn. After several hours he could take it no longer. He went over to Beckett's wagon and yelled at him.

He called Beckett some bad names and dared him to come out of the wagon.

It was known that you could make fun of the way Beckett looked but no one questioned his courage. Beckett stepped down on the ground and Braggs rushed him, knocking him down on the tailgate. Braggs stepped back and yelled, "Now I am going to kill you." He made a dive for Beckett and was met by the pick handle that Beckett had put on the tailgate. Braggs hit the ground with a loud yell and a thump. He was out cold.

People gathered around Beckett; they had no intention of letting Braggs do any thing to him. Braggs lay out cold. Someone brought a cloth and a pail of water and began to wash his face. They got him to just as the deputy arrived. The deputy took Braggs to jail when told what had happened.

Everyone thought it was over. That is, everyone but Braggs. He walked around with a bandage on his head for several weeks. Then, one day Beckett sat up with a sick friend and it was getting late when someone came to relieve him. He said he would be back in the morning but he never came.

The people wondered what had happened. If Beckett told you he would do something then everyone knew he would.

They were standing on the front porch, talking, when a boy came running up and said he saw Mister Beckett hanging in a tree. When they arrived, they found he had been dead for several hours.

At his funeral every one mourned him; they knew that the community had lost a good man. Time dragged by and no one was found and charged with the hanging. Beckett had been hung in a corner of the crossroad. They named it Beckett Corner.

Braggs walked around quiet, not speaking to anyone. Some said they heard that someone was out to get him. No one paid attention to him.

Then one of the people in the community had to get up early and make a trip to town. When he approached Beckett Corner he saw a man ride off down the road.

He could see his legs hanging down, his feet touching the ground. He would have sworn that it was Beckett. He shook his head and approached the intersection at the crossroad. He pulled his horse to a stop. There, hanging from the same limb that Beckett was hung, was Braggs.

Word went out that Beckett had come back and got his revenge. Everyone had known that Braggs had hung Beckett, but who had really hung Braggs? Could the figure that some say they have seen at Beckett Corners really be Beckett?

If you ever find out where Beckett Corner is located, come back at night and look for the tall man on the small mule. Some said he was there every night when some kind of event was being put on.

Lonie Adcock of Rome is a retired Rome Police Department lieutenant. His latest book is "Fact or Fiction."

GUEST COLUMN: Halloween prank backfire

Posted: Wednesday, October 26, 2016 6:00 am

I was reading the Rome News-Tribune when I noticed all the Halloween advertisements. When I grew up there was not much you could buy for Halloween. Most of the costumes were homemade by the parents of the kids. The grownups didn't do much about making up and wearing costumes. Then the parents of the small kids took them to Broad Street, where they could walk up and down being seen.

There was one Halloween that I will never forget as long as I live. It was in the late 1940s and I was living on Reece Street in North Rome. Duke, a friend that I ran with, lived up the street from me. Close to his house was a park where all the young people hung out. I had walked up to his house and was sitting on the porch with him when Carlton, another friend of ours, came up.

He sat down and asked, "What are we going to do to scare the girls tonight?" We looked at him and shook our heads.

"Do you remember the last time we tried to scare some of the girls," I asked Duke. "It was on the road below Coosa on the cut-off going to Summerville."

"I will never forget that," Duke said.

"I don't think that I will either."

Lonie Adcock

Lonie Adcock of Rome is a retired Rome Police Department lieutenant. His latest book is "Fact or Fiction."

We sat quiet for a while, not saying anything. Then a thought came to me. I told them of an old abandoned church in Little Texas Valley. It was falling in the last time that I had seen it. I told them we could go out and check on it. If it wasn't being used, we could fix it to where we would bring the girls. Duke and Carlton thought it was a good idea. We got in Duke's car and headed for the church.

The Church was run-down, the windows were broken and it only had one door — and that was hanging by a hinge. We got out and walked around the building, making sure there was a clear path around it. Then I moved the one-hinged door back against the wall to where it wouldn't fall on us and we went in.

When I stepped inside, a cold chill went down my back. I turned to look back at Duke and Carlton. They stood on the outside looking in at me. I motioned, saying, "Come on in, there's nothing here to hurt you. If we're going to bring them in here we need to move some of this stuff out of the way."

Rather hesitantly, they came in. There were torn-up benches and chairs scattered all over the floor. We began to move stuff to where we could get inside without falling over things. I went up to the pulpit and was amazed to see it stood there with no dust or anything on it. It was in good shape.

I remember telling Duke and Carlton that it looked as if someone had been using the pulpit. Carlton laughed and said, "Yeah, the ghosts have service here every Sunday night." Another cold chill went up my back and it felt like I was standing in an icebox.

I went and moved a chair from in front of where the side door used to be. Someone or something had taken the door and the facing. Seeing the window at the back had a board lying on the floor in front of it, I went over and picked it up. As I propped it up against the wall, I felt like someone or something was trying to make me leave the board on the floor. With the inside fixed to where we could get in, we left.

I left Duke and Carlton to round up the girls and went home, saying I would be back around six o'clock. But when I sat down to eat supper, I heard a car horn blow. I went to the door to find Duke and Carlton with a carload of girls. I told them to wait while I ate my supper but someone kept on blowing the horn, so I got up and went with them.

It was another one of them loads of more people than room. Somehow we were all piled in the car like sardines in a can. The car, a 1941 Hudson, had those small seats that would fold out from the back of the front seat. I remember there were 10 of us in the car — three boys and seven girls. We used to load up like that and go to the old Cedar Valley Drive In. It would cost you a dollar a car, just as many as you could get in it.

We drove Broad Street several times, until it was good and dark, then we headed for the church in the woods. With no lights but the headlight from the car, the church had a sinister look to it. When Duke turned off the headlight it was so dark that, as close as we were to the church, you just could make it out.

No one moved. Everyone sat perfectly still. "Oh, come on," I said, opening the car door and getting out. They all began to pile out, some falling on the ground.

"Like sardines in a can," I said, laughing as hard as I could.

The light that wasn't me

With everyone lined up, Duke was going to lead then inside. Carlton was going to bring up the rear, giving me a chance to go around back with my flashlight. I was going to make a groaning noise, then move the light around on the window. I never fully understood what happened, but after I helped get everyone inside and turned to go, I ran into a door. We had moved the door back against the wall that morning. But the door now was blocked by something and I couldn't get back outside.

I turned to look back at the others and it seemed that someone grabbed me by the arms and put me in a lock. I couldn't move. It was then that I realized everyone was quiet, not making a sound of any kind. They were watching a light in the corner near the window, where I was supposed to be.

Carlton let out a laugh. He thought the light was me with my flashlight. Then he turned and looked me straight in the face, and a groan went up from him.

"What is that light," asked Duke, who still thought it was me.

Carlton said, "Duke, Lonie is behind us."

It grew so quiet that the only thing you could hear was our heavy breathing. I remember being fascinated by the light, which seemed to dance around the floor. It was light blue, with a dark figure inside it. A sound like a giggle came from where the light was, then it disappeared and the room went dark.

Whatever had a hold of me had released my arms. I turned, taking my flashlight from my shirt pocket. Someone ran into the door and let out a loud yell. I found out later that it was Carlton who hit the door. Hit the door where there was no door. I shined my light on the spot. It was now a solid wall. I turned toward the side door, saying, "Come with me."

With everyone out ahead of me, I turned and shined the flashlight back across the room. The light was again in front of the window, moving around. Then someone or something snatched the flashlight out of my hand. That was my cue. I went through the door so fast I fell on the ground. I was up and around the building and getting into the car before I even realized it. Duke started the car and we got out of there in a hurry. No one said anything.

At that time there was a cafe on Martha Berry called Top Hat, or something similar to that. We stopped and went inside and sat down at a table. A waitress came over and took our order. No one spoke. It was plain to see that everyone was shook up.

I watched the girls and marveled at how quiet they were. I asked who had my flashlight, but no one said anything. "Someone took my flashlight from my hand while we were inside," I said. I looked around the table. They all said they hadn't taken my light. I let it slide for the time being. I could see that no one was in a talking mood.

We ate up and piled back into the car. Duke took all the girls home and let them out, then we went to the park and talked about what happened. We could not explain what had happened, but we agreed that our little prank had backfired on us.

Early the next morning I went up to Duke's house and we went back to the church. We wanted to see if we could figure out what had happened. I wanted to see if my flashlight was there. We pulled in and parked at the same place where we had the night before. The grass showed that we had been there. I walked over to the door. It was hanging on the one hinge, about half open.

I stepped around the door and went inside. I will always remember the cold chill that went from the top of my head to the bottom of my feet. I backed up, hitting the door. It made a noise and swung on the hinge. Duke grabbed it and shoved it back against the wall, the same way that we had the day before. I walked over to where I was the night before when someone took my light from my hand. It wasn't on the floor.

I began a search of the area, then noticed Duke staring at the pulpit. I walked over and there, laying on the pulpit, was my light. I reached over and picked it up. I could have sworn that I heard a giggle when my hand touched the light. I turned. "Let's get out of here."

We wasted no time getting into the car. As we pulled out, I looked back. I will always believe that the one-hinged door was hanging about half shut.

I don't remember ever trying to scare anyone after that. It was a short time later that I went into the Army. The mischievous boy was replaced by a man. But I will always look back and remember how a prank backfired on me. Did we really see a Halloween spirit, or was there someone playing a prank on us? It was one of those thing in life that can't be explained — so you file it in your memory and move on.

Lonie Adcock of Rome is a retired Rome Police Department lieutenant. His latest book is "Fact or Fiction."

GUEST COLUMN: Neighbors, ghosts and teenage rhymes: The joys of police work

Posted: Wednesday, November 2, 2016 6:00 am

In my 32 years on the Rome Police Department I dare say that I answered all kinds of calls. Some were funny and some were not. I will try to tell you some of the ones that I thought were funny. We'll leave the ones that were not to your imagination.

One of my cars received a call to East 15th Street. When I arrived I saw the officer standing on the porch, talking to a lady. It seemed that her next-door neighbor had caught her dog and tied him to a tree in her yard. He knocked on the door and when she came to the door, he wee-weed on her dog. He then untied the dog and went back and sat down on his porch.

I must have had a look on my face of disbelief, for the lady raised her right hand and said, "Officer, I swear on my mother's grave that what I said is the truth." I shook my head and told the lady that I would go over and talk to her neighbor.

Lonie Adcock

Lonie Adcock of Rome is a retired Rome Police Department lieutenant. His latest book is "Fact or Fiction."

The yard had a fence around it and you could not see what was in it until you got though the gate. It was one of the most beautiful yards that I have ever seen. It was full of flowers, some of which were large roses in many colors. The yard was a big flower the way it was laid out. I saw the old gentleman sitting in a swing, watching me as I approached.

I looked him over and drew the conclusion that he had to be 70 years old. "Officer," he said. "Did she tell you the whole story or did she just give you her version?" I told him what she had said and a smile came to his face. "Did she tell you that I said if she let her dog out again and he got in my yard that I would come over and wee wee on her?" I felt like laughing but managed to keep a straight face.

He got up and came down the steps, saying, "Follow me." I followed him to a spot where there was two dead rose bushes. "Officer, my wife made this garden. When she passed away, I made a vow to myself to keep her garden as long as I live. The woman has a fence to keep her dog in, but she turns him loose at night and he comes over and uses my garden for a toilet." I told him I would go back and have a talk with the lady.

As I started to open the gate I noticed a sign in the middle of a huge flower. It said Martha's Garden. I told the lady that she would have to keep her dog in her fence or the person to see her would be from the animal

GUEST COLUMN: The Whizz and I and the old man in a wheelchair

Posted: Wednesday, November 16, 2016 6:00 am

I was sitting here thinking about some of the things that people do. I often wondered why they want to be the way they are. You catch them doing it and they will stand flat-footed and lie to you.

Back in the early '60s I was riding in the patrol car with my partner The Whizz. We were working the south side of town and got a call to Branham Avenue about a man harassing some people. This was going to be one of those neighbor arguments. A call between neighbors is a hard call to settle. Both parties think they are right.

I started up to a house when The Whizz hollered at me, pointing to the house next door.

The house that I had started to was what we called a shotgun house — one where you walk in and go straight through from one room to the next. No hallway. An old man in a wheelchair sat on the porch.

Whizz got to the other house before I did. As I walked up, I heard one of the men on the porch call the man next door an

Lonie Adcock

Lonie Adcock of Rome is a retired Rome Police Department lieutenant. His latest book is "Fact or Fiction."

ugly word. I thought if they were complaining on the man in the wheelchair, they should have been ashamed.

On the porch was a woman who appeared to be in her 50s. There were three men: One appeared to be in his fifties, the other two in their 20s or early 30s. They were telling Whizz what all the old man had done to them. I told Whizz I was going over and talk to the old man next door.

The old man in the wheelchair watched me come up his driveway, then said "How are you officer?" I answered, "Fine, sir. And you?" He assured me he was doing fine then asked if there was something wrong next door. I watched his face as I explained that the people next door had made a complaint against him.

His face changed expression and he said, "What am I supposed to have done?" I told him that I hadn't heard it all. I wanted to hear what he had to say. He said they had dumped garbage in his back yard and he had called the police, and they had made them pick it up. He said that at night they would throw rocks against the side of his house.

I often wondered how someone could treat an old man in a wheelchair that way. I saw The Whizz getting into the patrol car. As I was getting in, I could tell by the look on his face that he had laid down the law to them.

Then we changed to the 11-to-7 shift and didn't have any calls to the house where the old man lived. We figured they had left him alone, but found out by talking to the fellows on the second shift that the quarrel was still going on. The latest thing that they done to the old man was tear down a section of his fence.

The Whizz and I made up our minds that we would keep a check on him.

The third shift on a Saturday night is busy up until late in the morning. After running all night, until somewhere around 2 o'clock, we thought we would ride by to check on the old man. I pulled up in front of the house and everything seemed to be okay. I started to drive off when Whizz said,"Stop! Stop!"

He jumped out and ran toward the house. I saw it then — the back of the house was on fire. Smoke was coming from under the house. I jumped out and ran to the door where Whizz was trying to get it open. I put my weight against it and it came off the hinges. We ran into the smoke-filled house, looking for the old man.

I heard a cry for help and ran into the room in the middle of the shotgun house. I yelled for The Whizz and, between the two of us, we got him into his wheelchair and out. I ran to the patrol car and called for dispatch to send the fire truck. Then we rolled the old man in his wheelchair out to the house next door, sat him on the porch and got back into the street to help the fire truck.

The fire was out in a short time and I walked to the back of the house. I heard one of the firemen say, "… a case of arson." It hit me that someone had tried to burn down the house with the old man in it.

I went over and told the fireman about the trouble that had been going on between the old man and the family next door. He and I walked back to the front, where by now a crowd had gathered. I saw the two young men from next door, standing and laughing. We walked over to them. The Whizz had joined us by that time.

When we walked up to them we got a whiff of gas. We knew then who had set the house on fire. We put the cuffs on the one who smelled like gas and put him in the back of the patrol car. The fire captain said they would get with a detective and work out a case against him.

I told the other one to go in the house and get his brother a pair of pants and shoes. When he got to headquarters he would be stripped of his clothing. The smell of gas on him was telling us what happened. We booked him in at headquarters with no doubt in our minds that the other one was also guilty

We were going back out on patrol when I realized that we had left the old man and his wheelchair sitting on the front porch of the house next door.

We drove back to find people walking around with flashlights, looking around the burned-out house. A woman came over to us and said they were looking for "Uncle John." I looked at the Whizz and began to laugh. I took the lady to the porch next door and sitting there asleep was Uncle John.

I remember the woman saying, "Glory be, he's safe." I explained to her that we had got him out of the house and in the excitement forgot him. She smiled and said, "All that matters is that Uncle John is safe. Thank you, thank you."

The Whizz and I left knowing that when the woman had said "thank you," she had paid us in full. We were glad that Uncle John was safe.

Lonie Adcock of Rome is a retired Rome Police Department lieutenant. His latest book is "Fact or Fiction."

GUEST COLUMN: As best as I can remember ...

Posted: Wednesday, November 30, 2016 5:30 am

As best as I can remember, I was somewhere between 5 and 6 years old when this took place.

We were living in Kingston when the farming got bad. The way I remember it, the landowner only wanted to let my father have half of the land that he had been farming.

My father found a farm close to White, Georgia, that was a better deal The man who owned the land got disabled, and he told my father he could farm as much as he wanted.

So from Kingston we moved to White.

The house was huge, with six rooms on the first floor and four on the second floor. My sisters went though and picked out their room. They wanted the second floor. My mother told me I would be on the first floor. I tried to get her to let me sleep on the second floor, but to no avail. I knew that they wanted on the second floor so they could giggle and laugh half the night. You know the way silly little girls do.

Things went good for a while, then bad things began to happen.

Lonie Adcock

Lonie Adcock of Rome is a retired Rome Police Department lieutenant. His latest book is "Fact or Fiction."

It started with me being accused of messing up the girls' room. They said that they made up their bed and I came up and threw the covers onto the floor. I tried to tell them that I had not done it.

Then, during supper when we all were at the table eating, we heard a noise that sounded like someone was dragging something down the hall. My father got up and went to check. He came back shaking his head. "You girls get up to your room and straighten it up." They looked at each other, then the oldest girl said, "We cleaned up our room and made up the bed this morning."

When the girls went up to their room, I followed. I peeped though the door and saw what our father had seen. The covers on the bed were thrown all around the room. I saw them look at me. I began to say, "I didn't do it" when my oldest sister came over and put her arms around me. The others followed, saying they were sorry they had accused me of messing up their room. They knew this time that I had not been in the room.

Back at the table I listened to them talk about the room and the bed covers thrown onto the floor. At that time I thought it was funny.

That night I went to bed in my room. One of the settees that my father made was in my room. The cushion on it was much softer than the mattress, and I would pull a piece of the covers from the bed and, with a pillow, would sleep on the settee.

I had just gotten asleep when the door opened and my sisters came into the room. They saw me on the settee and one of them whispered, "Can we sleep in your bed? We are afraid to stay in our room." I said yes, and snickered as they crawled into my bed.

I was awakened the next morning by my mother, who was demanding to know why the girls were in my bed and I was on the settee. She left the room saying, "I will see you young ladies at breakfast." I sniggered again and she said, "Young man, I will want to know why you are sleeping on the settee instead of the bed."

It worked out all right. The girls' bed and stuff was moved downstairs into the empty room. I would sleep on my bed instead of the settee. The door at the top of the stairs would be locked and no one would go there. From that moment on, the upstairs — and the soft settee — were off limits.

But one night I was lying in bed when I heard someone in the hallway. Thinking it was my father, and wanting a drink of water, I got up and looked out into the hall. I saw what I thought was my father go into the kitchen. So I went to the kitchen, where the water bucket was.

Back in those days, the hydrant was on the back porch and at night a fresh bucket of water was brought into the kitchen. There was always a dipper in the bucket. I didn't see my father in the kitchen so I went over to the bucket and got the dipper full of water.

I really don't know what happened next.

I turned the dipper up to take a drink when all the water poured out on me. I took a towel and tried to clean up the water. The front of my clothes were wet. I started back to my room when I thought I saw my father going toward the front of the hall. I couldn't let him see me wet, so I sneaked back into my room and hung up my clothes to dry. With my birthday suit on, I went back to bed.

The next morning, the subject was why was us kids were running up and down the hall making noise. My mother wanted to know who spilled water in the kitchen. I held up my hand. She never said anything else about the water. I told my father I had seen him in the hall. He assured me that he had not been in the hall at all last night. I wonder even now who I did see.

You could lay awake at night and hear things in that hall. One night at supper we heard something and, thinking it was the dog, my father went to check. He came back and said, "The dog is not in the house."

Another time, my mother and father had gone over to Cartersville for something and left us kids there alone. It was on a weekend and the crop had been gathered and we knew that they was ready to move out of the house that we were living in. Even though it was cool, us kids were out in the yard. It was starting to warm up and we were out under a tree where my father had placed some of his furniture.

I was rolling a tire around in the front yard when one of my sisters called me. I went to her and she pointed toward the upstairs window. I had rolled the tire before I saw what she was pointing at. The tire rolled down against the front porch and stood up. Nothing on either side to hold it up. There in the window was what looked like an Indian in full headdress. I don't recall ever playing with that tire again.

We gave our parents a blow by blow as to what we had seen in the window. We were informed that we would be moving from there in a couple of weeks. My mother always said that the house was haunted. I don't recall that my father ever said anything about it, but I remember that us kids were sure glad that we moved.

Was the house haunted or am I remembering things that didn't happen? I don't think I remember anything more clearly down though the years than the man looking out the upstairs window. I can still close my eyes and see him.

Lonie Adcock of Rome is a retired Rome Police Department lieutenant. His latest book is "Fact or Fiction."

You may have read some us these stories in the Newspaper at one time or another. They are taken from real life happenings and told as a story. These stories come from the time that was hard but good. A bowl of Grits for Breakfast and a bowl of Beans and Cornbread for supper. That was living high on the Hog ,even though you very seldom got any of the hog